TRACING YOUR
GREAT WAR ANCESTORS

The Egypt and Palestine Campaigns

FAMILY HISTORY FROM PEN & SWORD

TRACING YOUR GREAT WAR ANCESTORS

The Egypt and Palestine Campaigns

A Guide for Family Historians

Stuart Hadaway

Pen & Sword
FAMILY HISTORY

First published in Great Britain in 2017
PEN & SWORD FAMILY HISTORY
an imprint of
Pen & Sword Books Ltd
47 Church Street
Barnsley
South Yorkshire
S70 2AS

ISBN 978 147389 725 0

Typeset in Palatino and Optima by CHIC GRAPHICS

Printed and bound in England by
CPI Group (UK), Croydon, CR0 4YY

Pen & Sword Books Ltd incorporates the imprints of Pen & Sword
Archaeology, Atlas, Aviation, Battleground, Discovery, Family History,
History, Maritime, Military, Naval, Politics, Railways, Select, Social History,
Transport, True Crime, Claymore Press, Frontline Books, Leo Cooper,
Praetorian Press, Remember When, Seaforth Publishing and Wharncliffe.

For a complete list of Pen & Sword titles please contact
PEN & SWORD BOOKS LTD
47 Church Street, Barnsley, South Yorkshire, S70 2AS, England
E-mail: enquiries@pen-and-sword.co.uk
Website: www.pen-and-sword.co.uk

CONTENTS

ACKNOWLEDGEMENTS

My thanks go to Nina, for her usual support and patience, Dave Buttery for his map and assistance, and to Rupert Harding and Alison Miles at Pen & Sword. I would also like to thank David Tattersfield of the Western Front Association for his help and advice.

I would especially like to thank Graham Caldwell for his support and his characteristically uninhibited sharing of his extensive knowledge and expertise. Graham could easily be described as the Sherlock Holmes of First World War soldiers' records, and it is a rare case where he is not able to wrinkle out his man. He has kindly agreed that I can share his details here, and if you ever really hit a brick wall in your research, you can do no better than contact Graham for advice at: gljcaldwell@ozemail.co.au.

INTRODUCTION

If you ask most people about the First World War in the Middle East, they will mention either Lawrence of Arabia or Gallipoli. These two events are often misrepresented in themselves – the first as a blaze of adventure and glamour totally removed from the slaughter of the Western Front and the second as a tragic baptism of fire that is used, particularly by the Australians and New Zealanders, as a short-hand for youth and optimism being destroyed by incompetent generals. Both are equally misrepresentative when it comes to the war in the Middle East as a whole.

It is all too easy, especially given post-war events, to see the actions of the British Empire and other Allied nations in the Middle East as a grand, imperial land grab with little relevance to the wider war. The war in Egypt and Palestine was far from the main fight against Germany on the Western Front, and seems to bear little direct relevance to it. Instead, the fighting in Palestine and Syria led to the British and French in particular gaining control of this entire region as the Ottoman Empire was dissolved, dividing the land between them to their own best advantage.

But this view misses what a crucial campaign this was to the global war effort. There were several important strategic factors that made fighting in Egypt and Palestine important. One was the need to put pressure on Germany's weakest ally, the Ottoman Empire. Knocking them out of the war would be a material as well as a propaganda victory against the Germans, opening routes to attack another of Germany's allies, the Austro-Hungarian Empire, through the Balkans. It would also meet another strategic need, to ease the pressure on Russia and open a direct, year-round line of communication with that country.

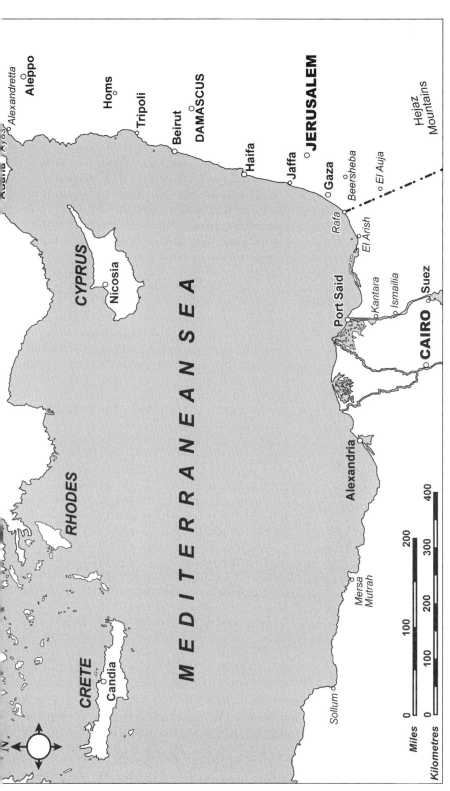

Map of the Egypt and Palestine theatre.

But the greatest strategic concern was the safety of the Suez Canal. Through the Canal flowed raw materials vital to the Allied war effort – feeding not only British war production, but also French and Italian too. This was also the shortest way to France for hundreds of thousands of troops from India, Australia and New Zealand. While ships could of course go around Africa, this took weeks longer. As the war progressed, not only did war production increase, but the shipping available decreased as losses mounted from the German submarine campaign. The faster a ship could reach port and unload, the faster it could be turned around and sent out for another cargo, and of course the faster those raw materials could reach the factories, making sure production levels met the ever increasing demands.

The Ottomans made several attempts to cut the Suez Canal in 1915 and 1916, and the great British offensive into Palestine in late 1917 forestalled another. However, large set-piece battles were fairly infrequent for the Egyptian Expeditionary Force (EEF), Britain's army in the theatre. Generally the tempo of operations was much lower in Egypt and Palestine than in France. However, the enemy, usually referred to a 'Johnny Turk' or 'Abdul', was a tough soldier and could be a formidable fighter. Coupled with the extensive problems of even existing in the conditions that prevailed in the theatre, this made campaigning in Egypt, Palestine and later Syria hard and dangerous work.

In Egypt and the Sinai Desert scorching heat coupled with lack of water, abrasive sand and masses of flies made life barely tolerable. In the trenches south of Gaza was more of the same, except that the troops were even further from any form of civilisation, with leave passes back to Egypt rare, and leave home to the UK almost unheard of except for officers. The advance from Gaza to Jerusalem in late 1917 took troops within a matter of weeks from the burning desert to high and freezing mountains in the middle of the winter rains. The advance into the Jordan Valley in 1918 brought even more oppressive heat as the men dropped below sea level, and also rampant malaria. The disease rate throughout the war was high in this theatre, with stomach diseases and skin complaints prevalent due to the lack of water and plagues of flies. Disease was a far bigger threat than enemy action, with more than ten times as many casualties caused by sickness. By 1918, only the worst cases were removed for treatment, with most men having to soldier on regardless.

In short, your ancestors who served in Egypt and Palestine (or, in the last few weeks of the war, Syria) played a vital role in securing eventual victory, while facing appalling conditions and, for the most part, receiving little appreciation or recognition. Hopefully, this book will help you explore that role and those conditions more fully, and build your own appreciation of their actions.

Before you go any further, there are two provisos the author would like to add. First, and most obviously, the information in this book is accurate at the time of going to print in mid-2017. The online genealogy services in particular update and change their services regularly, and it is always worth double-checking who provides what before making any decisions about who to subscribe to.

The second is more of a stylistic note. The records from the First World War period were kept on paper, often by busy and overworked clerks responsible for keeping the details on millions of men up to date. Mistakes were inevitably occasionally made, or particular files or sheets of paper lost or misfiled. Many Records of Service were destroyed during the Blitz in 1940, and other documents were also destroyed then or at other times. Therefore, almost every sentence in this book relating what information is on what record, or where a particular record can be found, should feature the word 'should' at least once. However, this would get repetitive, and so a single, massive 'should' is added here at the start instead.

Chapter 1

THE EGYPT AND PALESTINE CAMPAIGNS

1914

In July 1914, the countries of Europe began to slide towards war. The Ottoman Empire was initially outside the major alliances that bound Europe together, but on 1 August they signed a secret treaty to support Germany. Even so, they prevaricated about actually joining the war, and did not do so until the end of October, when their ships bombarded Russian ports. Russia immediately declared war, followed a few days later by Britain.

Britain had been hesitant to start a war with the Ottomans, although they believed one was coming. Egypt had been effectively ruled by Britain since the 1880s, primarily to ensure control of the Suez Canal, but the country remained technically part of the Ottoman Empire. Egypt was also largely Muslim, while the Sultan of the Ottoman Empire was also the Caliph, or nominal spiritual leader of Islam. Britain was worried (and would be for most of the war) that a war with the Ottomans would cause the millions of Muslims in Egypt, and across the British Empire in Africa and India, to rise up, although this proved an empty fear.

When war broke out, the British abandoned the Sinai Desert as being too big and empty to defend and withdrew to the Suez Canal, which was the vital link between Europe and the Far East and had to be defended at all costs. Even so, there were too few troops in Egypt to properly protect it, so Indian troops travelling to France were diverted to garrison the Canal. The 42nd (East Lancashire) Division of the Territorial Force (TF) was sent out from the UK, and

Jerusalem War Cemetery. The wall at the back lists all those who were killed but hav no known graves.

the thousands of new recruits from the Australian and New Zealand Army Corps (ANZAC) were also sent to Egypt. These British troops were not fit for front-line service yet, and the ANZAC troops (or 'Anzacs') had almost no training at all. Camps were set up in the Nile Delta to train these troops to be combat ready.

1915
Battle of the Suez Canal
In January 1915, the Ottomans gathered to attempt to cut the Suez Canal and perhaps even retake Egypt. They reached the Canal overnight on 2–3 February 1915, and attacked all along a 100-mile stretch of the Canal before dawn. The British had been warned weeks ago by aerial reconnaissance, and had prepared their defences. British and French warships had been moored in the Canal to use their big guns against the attackers, while the Indian and some Egyptian troops were well dug in and ready for them. By early afternoon, the Ottoman attack was in tatters and the force began to retreat. Out of a force of 12,000 men, only about 50 managed to cross the Canal, and over 1,000 were killed, wounded or captured.

The British forces, still under training and ill-equipped for expeditions into the desert, did not follow the retreating Ottomans. Small parties of Ottoman troops remained in the desert to harass the British positions on the Canal, and active British and Indian cavalry sections used to patrol on the eastern side of the Canal. However, for most of the rest of 1915 both sides were focused on the fighting at Gallipoli, and neither could spare the troops or resources needed to fight in the Sinai. (See Chapter 2, *Supporting Gallipoli*.)

The Senussi Campaign
The Senussi were a religious order based across North Africa, led by the Grand Senussi. The Ottomans and Germans applied much bribery and persuasion to try and get the Senussi to attack Egypt from their bases in Libya. The Ottomans and Germans provided them with heavy weapons – machine guns and artillery – as well as

Holyhead War Memorial, which lists the crew of HMS Tara, *who were held prisoner by the Senussi. There is also a plaque for Captain John Fox Russell RAMC, who won the VC in Palestine.*

the troops to operate them, and officers to act as advisors. Finally, on 5 November 1915, the Germans forced their hand, when the submarine *U-35* sank the British patrol vessel HMS *Tara*. Over ninety survivors were handed over to the Senussi, and *U-35* then bombarded the Egyptian Coastguard base at Sollum on the Libyan border.

Over the next few weeks, the Senussi pushed the British and Egyptians out of Sollum, Sidi Barani and Baqbaq. The British formed the Western Frontier Force from odd units across the country as a scratch force to stop the Senussi, and they pushed west to attack the Senussi. The first two actions went badly as British columns were ambushed near Wadi Senab on 11 December and Wadi Hasheifat on 13 December. In both cases the Senussi – born and bred desert fighters – hit the columns hard and, when the British slowly counterattacked, resisted until the British got too close and then melted back into the desert. Only on Christmas Day 1915 did the British get a clear victory, when at dawn they attacked and captured a Senussi camp at Jebel Medwa, near Wadi Majid, although most of the Senussi tribesmen escaped. A much more convincing victory followed on 23 January 1916, when the British routed a major Senussi force and captured their camp in a very hard-fought action at Halazin.

The British now began to benefit from the troops and resources being withdrawn from Gallipoli. They began to push back west along the coast, and attacked another significant Senussi camp at Aggagia on 26 February 1916. The British pushed the Senussi defenders back, and when they began to retreat the Queen's Own Dorset Yeomanry launched a devastating cavalry charge into their rear guard. Hundreds of Senussi were killed or taken prisoner, and large amounts of supplies captured. This broke the back of the Senussi resistance along the coast, and on 14 March Sollum was reoccupied. On 17 March, an armoured car column struck deep into the desert, covering 120 miles in a day to free the survivors from HMS *Tara*, who had been held in the desert for nineteen weeks in appalling conditions.

The Senussi on the coast had been defeated, but they still held many of the large oases in the Western Desert, including Siwa, Bahariya and Farafra. The British began active and aggressive patrols in the desert, using camel troops and armoured cars to travel through the empty wastelands between the oases, intercepting Senussi supply columns. The British worked with the Italians, who were also fighting the Senussi in Libya, to cut off their supplies and support. It was a slow business, but most of the Senussi forces began to be starved out, and in October and November 1916 almost all of the oases were abandoned by the Senussi and reoccupied by the British. Soon, only the force at Siwa, under the personal command of the Grand Senussi, remained. In early February 1917, a strong force of armoured cars was sent to Siwa, attacking at dawn on the 3rd. The Senussi forces were routed, and the Grand Senussi fled back into Libya. The Senussi signed a peace treaty with Britain and Italy in April 1917.

1916
Reorganisation
The forces that were withdrawn from Gallipoli in December 1915 and January 1916 were sent to Egypt to rest, be re-equipped and retrain before most were sent to France. Four infantry divisions, one cavalry division and some independent infantry and cavalry brigades were retained in Egypt, and these were designated the Egyptian Expeditionary Force (EEF) on 10 March 1916 under General Sir Archibald Murray.

Preparations had been going on for months to establish a major supply base at Kantara, on the Canal, and build a railway and a water pipeline from there into the Sinai Desert to supply a large British force, and in April 1916 the advance east began. The yeomanry cavalry of the 5th Mounted Brigade were sent out to seize the important wells around Qatia (or Katia) and Oghratina and develop them to supply the EEF. However, on 23 April 1916, a large Ottoman force, sent to attack the Suez Canal, came across the yeomanry and quickly surrounded them. The three regiments of yeomanry suffered terrible casualties, but stopped the bulk of the Ottoman forces attacking the Canal. Only one small Ottoman force made it near the Canal, and this was stopped by the Royal Scots Fusiliers at Dueidar. The Ottoman force retreated back towards Palestine, and the British pushed the 52nd (Lowland) Division and the Australian and New Zealand (A&NZ) Mounted Division out to seize the wells around Romani. Here, the infantry dug in while the cavalry began to aggressively patrol out into the desert.

Romani

The Ottomans made another attempt to attack the Suez Canal a few months later with around 16,000 men, running into the 14,000 men of the British forces at Romani on the night of 3–4 August 1916. The 52nd (Lowland) Division held a line of redoubts running north to south, while to the south of them the A&NZ Mounted Division held a totally unfortified line. In the dark the Ottomans advanced straight into the piquet line held by the Australian Light Horse (ALH), who, vastly outnumbered, staged a brilliant fighting withdrawal through the night and into the next day. Several times they were nearly overwhelmed, but they stopped once their line was at right angles to the Lowlanders, running east to west.

This was all pre-planned, and as the Ottomans began attacking north to try and break through the Australians, units of British and New Zealand cavalry attacked their open, western flank. This was followed that evening by a counter-attack by the Scots and Australians. There was hard fighting, but slowly the Ottomans were pushed back. The next morning the Ottoman forces broke and began to retreat, and British infantry and the cavalry attempted to mount a pursuit. However, the infantry (from the 42nd Division) suffered badly in the heat and soon stopped, while the cavalry were already exhausted from the previous day's fighting. The British lost about 300 men killed and 900 wounded; the Ottomans at least 1,400 killed and 4,000 taken prisoner.

The Ottomans were able to conduct a steady retreat east towards Palestine. They held various oases along the way, some of which the British attacked successfully, but most were too heavily defended.

British or Anzac cavalry would attack, but have to pull back in the face of heavy fire. While the cavalry went to water their horses and wait for infantry and artillery to come up, the Ottomans would pull back to the next oasis and prepare defences there. This pattern was repeated for several months.

To the Border of Palestine

By December 1916, the EEF was getting close to the border with Palestine. Two large Ottoman garrisons remained in their way, at El Magdhaba and El Magruntein. These were both attacked by the A&NZ Mounted Division and the Imperial Camel Corps, El Maghaba on 23 December 1916 and El Magruntein (also known as Rafa) on 9 January 1917. In both cases, the cavalry marched through the night to attack at dawn. It was necessary to capture the enemy posts, which were extremely well dug in and heavily defended, by nightfall, so that the horses could be watered. In both cases the fighting went on all day, and it was only at the very end of the day that the positions were captured. In fact at El Madghaba the final charge that won the day happened after the general commanding, Major General Harry Chauvel, had ordered the attack to break off. Combined, the A&NZ Mounted Division suffered about 100 men killed and 550 wounded across the 2 actions, whereas the Ottomans lost about 500 killed and 2,700 men taken prisoner.

The EEF now advanced into Palestine, and began to establish positions south of Gaza, a heavily fortified city on the coast that blocked the route north. At the same time, they continued to build the railway and pipeline across the desert, as well as develop water sources at El Arish to keep the army supplied.

1917

1st Battle of Gaza

On 26 March 1917, the EEF attempted to take Gaza. The battle was a fiasco, with almost no planning or reconnaissance beforehand, bad generalship and the blithe expectation that the Ottoman forces would try to run away.

The 53rd (Welsh) Division attacked the Gaza defences, particularly the heavily defended hill of Ali Muntar (and Green Hill and Clay Hill either side of it), to the south-east of Gaza and which dominated the city. This meant advancing for miles across flat and open country, and then navigating through tall, thick cactus hedges that marked allotments and gardens at the base of the hills. The division finally took Ali Muntar at dusk, but a breakdown in communications saw them being ordered to retreat. Although the order was reversed at midnight and the old Ottoman positions re-occupied, the exhausted troops were forced back by counter-attacks at dawn.

Meanwhile, the A&NZ Mounted Division, Imperial Mounted Division (British Yeomanry) and Imperial Camel Corps formed a cordon around the east and north of the city, holding off Ottoman reinforcements through the day. In the afternoon, the Anzacs were withdrawn to attack Gaza from the north, and managed to enter the city. However, with all of the cavalry forces isolated, outnumbered and threatened with being overrun, they were withdrawn overnight.

Next dawn, the 53rd Division, with the 54th (East Anglian) Division in support, tried to renew the attack but it was hopeless. They had lost 500 men killed, 3,000 wounded and 500 missing. That night they withdrew south to the Wadi Ghazze, where the main British lines were now established.

2nd Battle of Gaza

Three weeks later, the EEF attacked Gaza again. But the Ottomans had improved their defences, building a string of strong redoubts along the road heading south-east from Gaza towards Beersheba. The British were slightly more prepared, with more troops and a handful of tanks. They even had some poison gas shells, although when used the gas simply evaporated in the heat. Despite these new weapons, the attack was still poorly planned and lacked proper support.

While the 53rd (Welsh) Division attacked up the coast, the 52nd (Lowland) Division attacked Ali Muntar and Gaza, and the

HMLS 'Otazel' (pronounced 'Ot as 'Ell), one of the tanks used at Gaza.

54th (East Anglian) Division attacked the redoubts along the Gaza–Beersheba road. Out on the eastern flank the cavalry divisions attacked some of the furthest redoubts, and also skirmished with Ottoman cavalry coming out of Beersheba.

Again the attacks failed. The tanks were mostly knocked out very quickly, and although the British managed to enter some of the redoubts, the Ottomans staged strong and efficient counter-attacks to push them back out. The attack ended with the British losing 500 men killed, 4,400 wounded and over 1,500 missing.

Summer

After the second failure to take Gaza, the EEF dug in just south of the city. Trench systems grew up south and south-east of Gaza, but as the line went east it developed into a series of outposts instead of continuous lines. Cavalry patrols covered the eastern, desert flank, regularly skirmishing with Ottoman patrols. The infantry held the trenches, usually for three or four weeks at a time, and both sides actively patrolled no-man's-land and raided the other side's trenches and posts.

On 27 June 1917, General Murray was replaced by General Sir Edmund Allenby. With him came reinforcements (including two whole divisions – the 10th (Irish) and 60th (London) from Salonika, while two more – the 74th (Yeomanry) and 75th – were raised in Egypt), more and better artillery, more and better aircraft, and a new, positive attitude. He increased the rate of retraining the EEF in new techniques, and reorganised the army into three Corps. The 10th (Irish), 53rd (Welsh), 60th (London) and 74th (Yeomanry) Divisions formed XX Corps. The 52nd (Lowland), 54th (East Anglian) and 75th Divisions formed XXI Corps. The cavalry were reorganised into three divisions – the A&NZ, Imperial and Australian Mounted Divisions – and gathered together into the Desert Mounted Corps.

(The 74th (Yeomanry) Division, incidentally, was infantry despite being made up of erstwhile cavalry units. Many yeomanry units were sent to Gallipoli to fight on foot, leaving their horses in Egypt. When they returned they were kept as infantry and eventually formed into the 74th Division, which adopted the symbol of a broken spur as its badge.)

Allenby developed a new plan to break through the Ottoman lines, attacking Beersheba and then 'rolling up' the Ottoman line from the east. Once the defensive line was broken he would take the EEF north to capture Jerusalem, about 50 miles (80km) away in the Judean Mountains. The timings would be tricky; keeping his forces supplied would be hard work and require careful balancing of limited resources, especially trucks and camels. He also had to be careful of the rainy season, which would begin in November and bring months of heavy rainfall in the mountains, turning currently dry wadis into raging currents and large areas of the coastal plains into swamps.

3rd Battle of Gaza
The biggest British artillery bombardment of the war outside France

A 60lb field gun, used to batter Ottoman defences on the Gaza–Beersheba line.

or Belgium began on 27 October 1917, with warships of the Royal Navy (RN) as well as the army pounding the Ottoman defences at Gaza. While this distracted Ottoman attention, XX Corps and the Desert Mounted Corps secretly moved onto the desert flank and attacked Beersheba on 31 October. The day went slowly, with the Ottomans as usual performing very well in strong defensive positions, but near dusk a charge by the ALH captured the town. The troops there then paused until 3 November before striking to the north and to the west to destroy the Ottoman defences along the Gaza–Beersheba road. In particular, it was important to take Tel el Sheria, which was the main supply and communications hub for the whole line, and which was captured on 7 November. Meanwhile,

XXI Corps attacked Gaza on 2 November, taking several days to work through the enemy defences. On 7 November, the Ottomans left Gaza, and the race to Jerusalem began.

The Ottomans now pulled back in good order. Allenby struggled to catch and destroy them, although various units and rear guards were over-run or surrendered. The British advance was switched between the two infantry Corps as each in turn became exhausted, rested and was resupplied, and then took to the front line again, while the Desert Mounted Corps moved backwards and forwards across the country to fight where needed. Allenby was an excellent delegator. He gave his subordinates their broad objectives, and then left them (with their expert knowledge of their own troops and the country ahead of them) to meet those objectives as they saw fit. Meanwhile, Allenby focused on the 'big picture' and on keeping the supplies flowing, which became increasingly difficult as the EEF advanced further and further from their original lines. The camel trains of the Egyptian Labour Corps' Camel Transport Corps were invaluable.

The Ottomans made several stands, and had to be forced out of strong defensive positions around El Mughar and El Tine before the crucial supply base at Junction Station was captured on 14 November. After a few days' rest, Allenby launched his forces forward again on 18 November, with XX Corps going north to capture the port at Jaffa (easing the supply problems) and XXI Corps heading east into the Judean Mountains, towards Jerusalem. In the Mountains conditions were harsh, as the rains had now started and the men were ill-equipped to deal with such cold and wet conditions. On 21 November they attacked and took Nabi Samwil, a mountain top that overlooks the roads into Jerusalem, although there would be bitter fighting here for weeks afterwards as the Ottomans tried to retake it. Elsewhere, the British started moving north of Jerusalem but were blocked, and then on 27 November the Ottomans staged a counter-attack that almost threw the British back. Allenby now paused and rotated his Corps to bring fresher men into the mountains.

Camel trains of the Egyptian Labour Corps played a vital role in keeping the troops supplied.

The attack restarted on 8 December 1917, and that night the Ottomans evacuated Jerusalem, giving it up without a fight to prevent damage to the historic city. On 9 December British troops entered, and on 11 December, Allenby officially accepted the surrender. Meanwhile, British forces continued to push north and east of the city. The Ottomans staged a major counter-attack from the north on 27 December, which the British stopped and then pushed back, capturing more ground. On 30 December operations ceased.

On the coast, where the landscape was turning into a swamp, the British had tried to push across the Nahr el Auja River on 24 November, but had been forced back the next day. On 20 December they crossed again, and over the next couple of days secured a stretch of land on the northern side, making Jaffa secure. The offensive had cost the British 21,000 casualties, many to the disease, weather and exhaustion, and the Ottomans 28,000 men, but had seen the British advance 50 miles.

1918
Into the Jordan Valley
On 19 February 1918, the fighting restarted as XX Corps advanced into the Jordan Valley. On 21 February they captured Jericho. Now in the Jordan Valley, the EEF could try to link up with the Arab forces revolting against the Ottomans (see p. 17 below) to the east. From 8 March, a series of attacks along the lines north of Jerusalem pushed the Ottomans back a short distance.

Cross-Jordan Raids
On 21 March 1918 the British struck east across the River Jordan towards Es Salt and Amman. Their aim was to take Amman, and cut the Ottoman Hejaz Railway, the supply line south into the Arab Peninsula. Heavy rains slowed the advance through the already difficult mountain passes, and the attack on Amman itself did not start until 30 March. By then, Ottoman reinforcements had been brought in, and the attack failed. Under increasing counter-attacks, the British retreated back across the Jordan on 2 April, leaving a bridgehead east of the river at Ghoraniyeh. On 11–12 April the Ottomans attacked the bridgehead without success.

On 30 April the British struck across the Jordan again, but the Ottomans had greatly strengthened their defences, and the attacking forces only got as far as Es Salt. On 4 May the British withdrew again across the Jordan.

Summer
On 21 March 1918 the Germans had broken through on the Western Front, and within weeks British troops were being stripped out of Palestine to be sent to France. They were replaced by Indian troops sent out directly from India, with little or no combat experience. The 52nd (Lowland) and 74th (Yeomanry) Divisions went as a whole,

being replaced by the 3rd (Lahore) and 7th (Meerut) Divisions. Dozens of infantry battalions and numerous Yeomanry regiments, artillery batteries and machine-gun companies had also been withdrawn, and were slowly replaced by Indian units. All of the brigades in every British infantry division were reorganised with one British battalion and three Indian ones (except the 54th (East Anglian) Division, which remained fully British). The cavalry were also reorganised with one British regiment and two Indian regiments in most brigades. The old Yeomanry Division was broken up to supply the British troops for the newly formed 4th and 5th Cavalry Divisions.

Most troops were rotated through the Jordan Valley over the summer of 1918, where the heat and atmosphere were stifling and malaria rife. It was a deeply unpleasant experience, and sickness rates reached such a high level that the less severe cases had to remain on duty, otherwise the EEF would not have had enough troops to hold the line. Skirmishing and raiding by both sides went on in the Valley.

Between June and August a series of raids and small attacks were also made on the coastal flank, to either gain valuable ground or test the standards of the Indian troops. In September preparations began for the next big offensive. Troops were gathered on the coastal flank, while an elaborate deception plan was put in place to fool the Ottomans into thinking the attack would come in the Jordan Valley.

Battle of Megiddo

On 19 September 1918, Allenby launched an attack on the coastal plain of Palestine, directed north towards the Plain of Megiddo (known in the Bible as the Plain of Armageddon). The British broke through the poorly supplied and badly equipped Ottoman troops and forced them into retreat within hours. The infantry followed up and defeated Ottoman forces at the Battles of Sharon and Mount Ephraim on 20 September, after which the battle became a mostly cavalry affair. Only the cavalry could move fast enough to catch the retreating enemy, although the Royal Air Force (RAF, formed from the Royal Flying Corps (RFC) and Royal Naval Air Service (RNAS) in April 1918) also played an important role in locating and destroying Ottoman units. In particular, they patrolled and blocked the lines of retreat east towards the Jordan Valley, and even caught and destroyed by bombing the remains of the Ottoman 7th Army in the Wadi Fara on 21 September. On 23 September Indian cavalry captured the port at Haifa, and on the following day the ALH reached the Sea of Galilee.

The campaign was hard work, with the troops advancing hard and fast, living rough and frequently being beyond the reach of their own supply lines. Ottoman forces surrendered in droves, with sometimes a few dozen cavalrymen herding hundreds or thousands of prisoners back towards British lines.

The advance now carried on north into Syria, and on 1 October, Damascus was captured. On 25 October, Arab forces reached Aleppo, and the British arrived the following day. On 30 October, the Ottoman Empire surrendered.

THE ARAB REVOLT

Little has been said so far about the Arab Revolt, begun by the Emir of Mecca, Sharif Husein ibn Ali, in the Arab Peninsula in June 1916. It is most famous now as the theatre of T.E. Lawrence 'of Arabia', sent out to act as an advisor to the Arabs in January 1917. He masterminded one of the early victories, the capture of the port of Wejh at a time when the whole Revolt was about to fail, but he was still only one of many British advisors and officers involved. In Arabia, the Revolt was little more than a sideshow; a drain on Ottoman military resources and a political embarrassment, but no major threat.

However, Husein wanted to spread his influence north across all of the Arab nations, and Lawrence made this possible by leading a force to capture of the port of Aqaba at the top of the Red Sea in July 1917. This opened the route north to the Arabs. Over the following months they made slow progress in pushing the Ottoman forces back, but once the British offensive in southern Palestine was successful they advanced on the Dead Sea. In early 1918 they fought a few actions around the Dead Sea, but then failed to make any contribution when the British tried to capture Amman. By this time, significant numbers of British troops were helping the Arabs, including detachments from the RFC, armoured cars and camel troops.

Only in the final offensive did the Arabs really make a difference to the EEF's campaigns, attacking north in tandem with the British. They helped keep the Ottoman forces in the Jordan Valley from reinforcing the coastal areas, and then pushed them back north. Later, they swung across into Syria, reaching Aleppo to claim control of the whole region for the Arabs. This claim was later overruled at the Paris Peace Conference, and the region was divided. Britain received the Mandate for governing Palestine, while the French took over Syria.

LOGISTICS

It is worth looking very briefly at the question of logistics – the science (and sometimes art) of keeping an army supplied with everything it needed while fighting in an inhospitable land, far from home. Some of these problems – obtaining food and, particularly, water, for example – will be running themes in this book, and others will be mentioned in their place. But it would be good to emphasise here that logistics were a constant, daily struggle involving thousands of men doing unglamorous jobs in depots, workshops and warehouses, for whom just one mistake could have serious repercussions.

By the end of October 1918, the EEF occupied about 120,000km^2 /46,000 square miles of enemy territory. Across that area a constant stream of food had to be kept up for some 341,000 British and Indian troops (some of the latter having specific religious or cultural dietary requirements), 133,000 Egyptians, 160,000 animals and around 90,000 Ottoman prisoners. Water for this force would be around 1.6 million gallons/7.3 million litres every single day. Of the other supplies needing to be distributed to keep those units functioning, ammunition alone amounted to 250 tons every single day. In the average week, the army would also have to distribute to the correct recipients over 7,000 bags of mail, a task they took very seriously due to the huge importance that receiving news from home had on the morale of the troops. In return, they had to collect over 550,000 letters to be sent home, and about 180,000 for elsewhere in EEF or the occupied territories per week.

These men were spread over vast areas of mountain and plain across Syria, Palestine and the Trans-Jordan, with almost no railways and very few roads worth the name. The ground was so rough that the 5,000 or so trucks used by the EEF wore out their tyres after an average of only 700 miles (the average in France was 10,000 miles). Repairing and maintaining those vehicles, plus the thousands of wagons, limbers and other wheeled transport, was a gargantuan task by itself.

Much of the transport and logistics relied on Egyptian labourers. The Egyptian Labour Corps (ELC) was initially made up of volunteers, but by 1918 the men were conscripted due to the importance of their work, and reached a strength of just over 100,000 by the end of the war. They worked on building roads and railways, laying water pipelines and digging wells, carrying loads and digging trenches. Not all were just labourers, and craftsmen in the ELC manufactured or repaired all manner of equipment and components. A sub-unit, the Camel Transport Corps, handled the nearly 26,000 camels on which the army relied for most of the forward supply work, carrying a wide variety of supplies from railheads and dumps up to the front-line units. Often looked down upon, abused or the subjects of casual racism, without these men the EEF simply could not have operated.

The same goes for the tens of thousands of support troops who were often abused or denigrated for apparently shirking the fighting or somehow not doing their bit, or were blamed whenever the supply system did not work as it should. In fact, those men should be credited with doing a magnificent job, without which the EEF simply would not have been able to operate.

INNOCENTS ABROAD

The vast majority of the men who served in this theatre came ashore in Alexandria or Port Said. Before 1916 most came by ship all the way from the UK, and after 1916 many may have travelled across France before embarking on their troopships. By either route, their convoy may have paused at Malta, but probably without giving anyone the chance to go ashore. Conditions on these troopships could be grim. Many were nothing more than converted merchant ships, which had never been intended to carry so many passengers, leaving both the sanitary and the messing facilities greatly lacking. Even purpose-built troopships were usually packed far beyond their normal capacity. Anthony Bluett of the Honourable Artillery Company sailed out in early 1915 in:

> A troopship packed to three or four times its normal peace-time capacity; where men slept on the floors, on mess-tables, and in hammocks so closely slung that once you were in it was literally impossible to get out until the whole row was ready to move; and where we were given food (!) cooked and served under conditions so revolting as to turn the stomach at the bare sight of it. (A. Bluett, *A Gunner's Crusade* (n.p., Leonaur Ltd, 2007), p. 11)

The routine on board could be monotonous as there was little space for recreational facilities, although some found the experience itself invigorating. Private William Lindsay of the Royal Scots recalled the daily experience in a letter:

> Reveille 5, hammocks stowed 6. Breakfast 6.45. Parade 10–11. Dinner 11.45. 2–2.30 parade. 4.45 tea. 9 bed. There are two orderlies for each table. They draw the food, wash the dishes and clean up . . . The men are all in the best of spirits and time does not hang heavily on our hands for there is usually something strange to see . . .

British soldiers enjoying Egyptian coffee at a road-side cafe in Cairo.

For most men, their first experience of a truly foreign country would have been the sights, sounds and smells of the markets and alleyways of Egypt.

To men who had probably never travelled far from their home town, and who did not have the benefit of television and colour media as we do today, the impact of such a vibrant and exotic experience must have been great. On the troopships many men were cautioned about the dangers of local food, drink and women, although the latter warnings at least were frequently ignored. For young men let loose for the first time on their own in a faraway land, the temptations of local bars were often too much to resist. The alcohol in Egypt was frequently 'homebrewed', strong and full of impurities that had a powerful effect even on seasoned drinkers. Drunken soldiers were often then lured into upstairs rooms or local brothels, and particularly in 1914 and 1915 venereal diseases were a major drain on army manpower. Harsh measures had to be put into place, such as forfeiting men's pay while they were in hospital, and a drastic increase in the numbers of military police. However, as the army moved into the desert and far from the 'pyramids and fleshpots' of Egypt the problems with drunkenness and VD decreased greatly.

Men usually spent at least a week in Alexandria or near Cairo to acclimatise to the heat, and sometimes much longer. Troops would go through drill and exercises in the early morning and late afternoon, gradually doing more during the main heat of the day. Most soldiers would have been issued light 'khaki drill' uniforms – cotton instead of woollen serge – and pith helmets before arriving in the country, but others would only have received them once in Egypt. Private John Taberner of the Manchester Regiment was one of the first to arrive, in September 1914. He found he had to carry all of his kit from the docks to Mustapha Barracks:

You have no idea how much work there is to march with full pack on from the boat including the army Great Coat which is enough for any man by itself . . . The sun was scorching & we had to march to the fort without a stop. Sweat was running off our faces & hands in a continual stream . . . We are still in the same heavy uniform we had in England which is worse than cruelty to animals although we are expecting new thin uniforms any moment . . . The army shirts are thick woollen & the socks are of that coarse wool & are too thick for this climate.

Private George Tuttlebee, 1/4th Battalion, Royal Sussex Regiment, arrived in Egypt three years later on 31 May 1917, by which time the army was better organised. His diary shows the gradual increase in activity over his first week:

Monday, 4th June
Reveille at 5.30 and breakfast at 6, then got ready to parade for route march at 9 o'clock. It was very hot marching and the flowers in the gardens of the houses were magnificent. The bazaars had all kinds of things for sale which were made of some of the brightest materials. When we arrived back we had finished parades for the day.

Tuesday, 5th June
Reveille at 5.30. Breakfast at 6. We parade at 8 o'clock to change our unserviceable clothing. I then had a dip in the sea before dinner. At 2 o'clock we were paid out. I received 60 piastres also a pass to go into Alexandria. I went into Kitchener's Home and had tea then took the train into Alexandria and spent the evening there, also had my photo taken. Arrived back in camp about 9 o'clock.

Wednesday, June 6th
Reveille at 5.30. Breakfast at 6 and parade at ¼ to 8 for a bath and medical inspection at 9.30, dinner at 12 o'clock and at ¼ to 2 paraded for bayonet practice which lasted for about ½ an hour. Tea was at ¼ to 5 after which I went to the YMCA and wrote letters.

Thursday, June 7th
Paraded at 9 o'clock for route march and arrived back at 10 o'clock. I then had a dip in the sea and had a rest until 12 o'clock when we had dinner. In the afternoon I wrote letters and at 3.30 had C.O.'s parade which lasted up till 5 o'clock and we were then finished for the day.

After a week or two in the camps of Egypt, troops would face a long march out to their units in the Sinai, or later a train journey up into Palestine.

A convalescing Australian (in his blue hospital uniform) fraternising with an Egyptian.

Chapter 2

GETTING STARTED

There are so many companies and websites that offer genealogical military records for the First World War that the range can be quite bewildering. In many ways your choice will be based on your existing subscriptions with such sites. To begin with at least it is perhaps most important to go with the sites you know, or to be more precise the sites whose search engines you are most used to!

The main sites that will be mentioned here are: Ancestry UK (www.ancestry.co.uk), Find My Past (www.findmypast.co.uk), The Genealogist (www.thegenealogist.co.uk), Naval & Military Archive (www.nmarchive.com), and Forces War Records (www.forces-war-records.co.uk). Most of the original records are held by The National Archives (TNA) at Kew, and can also be accessed through them. Their catalogue can be found at: http://discovery.nationalarchives. gov.uk.

The basic starting points are the same as for any genealogical research: talk to relatives to see what is already known about the person (although, as ever, take this with a pinch of salt to allow for the vagaries of human memory) and gather existing documents and artefacts. From these, you need to establish their basic military identifying data set: name, rank and number.

First, you will need to establish their proper full name as well as the one they commonly used. While a few people signed up under false names, many used the opportunity to ditch unpopular first names and use their middle names instead, or equally signed up under their proper names whereas their families knew them by a nickname. The name will appear on any paperwork relating to their service – letters, pay book, pension forms – or on their medals, albeit only as initials and surname. It is much easier to trace someone if they were killed, as the name will appear on either their 'death penny' (a bronze plaque sent, with a certificate, to the relatives of the fallen) or within the Commonwealth War Graves Commission's (CWGC) Roll of Honour on their website.

SERVICE NUMBERS

After name, the most important elements are the individual's service numbers and unit. The service number was supposed to be the unique identifier of each man within his wider unit (although, as we shall see, it was not necessarily). There may well be several men in the same unit with the same name – in fact this was almost guaranteed in Welsh, Irish or Scottish units – and so the number told them apart. It was given to a man on his actually reporting for service rather than on his attestation. His attestation came when the man physically reported to a recruiting office, either as a volunteer or, from January 1916, as a conscript. That was when the basic paperwork on the individual and their background was filled in, as well as a medical examination carried out. However, most recruits would then be sent home again to await the call to report for duty. When the next basic training course was about to begin, he would be called back to actually join the army properly, be issued his kit and start training. It was at that point that the number was issued.

The service number for other ranks should appear on the paperwork or medals referred to above, and will probably also appear on the CWGC listing for someone. Each regiment was responsible for issuing numbers to all of their battalions (terms explained in Chapter 6, Researching Units). Unfortunately, the system was not uniformly applied, and there are some pitfalls and peculiarities with numbers. Sometimes regiments gave each battalion a block of numbers to use, and sometimes the regiments gave men the next available number from the central list regardless of battalion. Some battalions just assigned their own numbers irrespective of what the regiment said. When a man changed unit,

NOTHING is to be written on this side except the date and signature of the sender. Sentences not required may be erased. If anything else is added the post card will be destroyed.

[Postage must be prepaid on any letter or post card addressed to the sender of this card.]

I am quite well.

~~I have been admitted into hospital~~

{ sick ~~and am going on well,~~

{ wounded } ~~and hope to be discharged soon.~~

~~I am being sent down to the base.~~

~~I have received your~~ { ~~letter dated~~ ____

{ ~~telegram ,,~~ ____

{ ~~parcel ,,~~ ____

Letter follows at first opportunity.

~~I have received no letter from you~~

{ ~~lately~~ ____

{ ~~for a long time.~~

Signature } *y Smith*
only

Date _10th Aug 1915_

Wt. W34977293 29248. 6000m. S-p. O. & Co., Grange Mills, S.W.

A field service postcard, used when paper or time were short.

he changed his number as well. This means that there would have been dozens of soldiers across the army with the number 4035, for example. Only in 1920 was the system standardised and everyone received a new number, one that was unique across the whole army. Therefore, it is possible (if very unlikely) for two people with the same or very similar names to have the same number as well. It also means that some men could be recorded on certain records under two or even more different numbers.

The numbers can provide some assistance by themselves. Low numbers indicate the soldier joined up relatively soon after the raising of their battalion. Numbers sometimes have lettered prefixes as well which can help, although these can equally confuse. For war-time enlistees, for example, 'G' was a common pre-fix used by many Home Counties regiments, while 'L' was used by the Royal Artillery. While some regiments had their own unique prefix, some letters were used by many different units or branches. 'S', for example, was used by the Royal Artillery, the Royal Army Medical Corps, some of the Highland Regiments, the Rifle Brigade, the Royal Munster Fusiliers, the Army Ordnance Corps and some parts of the Army Service Corps. While most of these units used it for war-time enlistees, others also used it for pre-war members as well. Thankfully, there is an excellent website – armyservicenumbers. blogspot.co.uk – that provides detailed guidance on this and many other service-number related issues.

If your relative's Record of Service has been destroyed (see Chapter 4, Researching British and Dominion Soldiers), you can use service numbers to narrow down when he actually joined the army. By looking for surviving records of men in the same unit with similar numbers, you can work out a time frame of sometimes just a few days for when he may have reported for duty.

Officers did not have service numbers. Instead, when numbers are given for officers these are actually the 'long numbers' that are the references used for their personnel files at the War Office. Therefore, they can still be useful for confirming identities, perhaps even more so as they are unique.

Between them, with all of the exceptions and provisos given above, names and numbers are still the best guarantee that the John William Finch that you've found the records for is *your* John William Finch.

The units your ancestor served with can be obtained from similar records, and often appear as some form of abbreviation. These are far too numerous to list in a work like this, but a simple Internet search should help. Once you have the unit, you can start unpicking exactly what your relative did, when and where. This will be explored more in Chapter 6.

RANKS

The final piece of the personal data list is rank, although to begin with it is only really necessary to know whether they were an officer or in the ranks, and then only because officers' and other ranks' records are kept in separate series at TNA. Even if you are accessing these records through one of the online record providers, this original filing system is still of importance.

An officer is someone of a commissioned rank, given authority by the King to command units in his army. The lowest is a Second Lieutenant, usually responsible for a platoon of about fifty men, with a Lieutenant (with much the same responsibilities but more seniority) above him, and then a Captain commanding four platoons together as a company. These were by far the most common officer ranks, and although the examples of their responsibilities here are for an infantry officer (the most common type – the organisation of other types of unit are discussed in Chapter 6) the same ranks were also used in comparable roles for units of cavalry, and specialist troops such as artillery, engineers, logistics and the RFC.

The 'other ranks' were anyone who was not an officer. These included 'non-commissioned officers' or NCOs, such as Lance Corporal, Corporal and Sergeant who held subordinate commands within platoons, and various types of Sergeant Major (who were classed as 'Warrant Officers'), who were generally in a more administrative role. As with the officers, these ranks were broadly the same across most of the branches, except the artillery that used the term Bombardier instead of Corporal.

The lowest rank was the Private soldier, and here the terms did often change across branches. The cavalry called them Troopers, although they remained officially Privates and were just known as Troopers. In the Royal Engineers they were Sappers, in the Royal

Artillery they were Gunners and in the RFC they were Airmen, among many other variations. Even within the infantry, different regiments had their own customs, with Guardsmen, Fusiliers and Riflemen, for example, all making their appearance.

Ranks can, therefore, help point you in the right direction for the unit in which your ancestor served, and of course are an important piece of the overall picture of what your relative experienced. However, this is less important than the other elements when it comes to tracking individuals down in the records.

MEDAL INDEX CARDS AND ROLLS

If your ancestor survived the war, and you do not have any handy paperwork or medals to provide the basic data list, then unfortunately you will have to do it the hard way. The best sources are now the medal rolls and their index cards, compiled to ensure that each man received the correct campaign medals at the end of the war. There were four of these:

- 1914 Star: For personnel who served in France or Belgium between 4 August and 22 November 1914, covering the crucial early battles on the Western Front.
- 1914–15 Star: This one is more relevant to Egypt and Palestine, as it was for all men who served in an overseas theatre before 31 December 1915. There were plans originally for a separate Gallipoli Star, but this was eventually included in the 1914–15 Star.
- British War Medal: This was awarded to all personnel who had served in the armed forces between 5 August 1914 and 11 November 1918. Originally, there were going to be individual battle and campaign clasps, but the provisional lists drawn up included sixty-eight clasps for the RN and seventy-nine for the army! The idea was abandoned post-war when the practicalities of the scheme were examined, but it is a shame as it would have made tracing your ancestor's service a lot easier.
- Victory Medal: This had the same basic criteria as the British War Medal, but was issued across almost all of the victorious Allied

Men of the ALH wait in an ambush in the desert.

countries – 14.5 million were issued in all. The obverse of the medals of all nations except Japan and Siam showed a winged figure of 'victory', with each country modifying the figure to match their own cultural images.

Medal Index Cards include the basic details on each man such as rank, service number and the units they served with, complete with dates. Unfortunately, usually only the higher unit is recorded on the cards, i.e. the regiment or corps, and the exact battalion or sub-unit is only occasionally recorded. They then list the medals to which that individual was entitled.

Up until the end of 1915 the Medal Index Cards consistently list the theatres (i.e. France, Gallipoli, Egypt) in which they first served and the date of their first entry into that theatre. After the end of 1915, this information is seldom recorded, although a few still have it.

The theatre was recorded by name or through a code number: '3' was used for Egypt from the start of the war until the end of 1915. It is also worth noting that '2' meant Gallipoli, and that many men who served in the Dardanelles transited briefly through Egypt, or were taken to Egypt if they were evacuated as sick or wounded. Almost all of the forces who served in Gallipoli were withdrawn to Egypt at the end of the campaign even if they were then sent on to France or elsewhere.

From 1 January to 18/19 March 1916, the code '4a' was used for Egypt, after which '4b' was used. Also of possible interest are some of the '6' series of numbers: '6a' indicated service in the Hejaz region (on the western side of the Arab Peninsula), '6e' South West Arabia and '6f' Aden.

It is worth remembering that the campaign information is supposed to be for the first entry into their first overseas campaign. Most of the men who went on to serve in Palestine from 1917 onwards, and in the Jordan Valley and Syria from 1918, entered the theatre through Alexandria or Port Said, and so the code given for them would still be Egypt.

The copies of the index cards at TNA (in series WO 372) are on microfiche and in black and white, and can be searched for through their 'Discovery' online catalogue for free, although you will need to pay to download a digital image of the record itself. The originals were disposed of in 2005 and rescued from destruction by the Western Front Association (WFA). They have made scans of both sides of the cards (the backs occasionally contain added details) and these are available either directly from the WFA (more details on their services are given in the 'Pension Cards' section of Chapter 4) and also through Ancestry. These cards are an index for the medal rolls, which usually give the same information but occasionally have a detail that the index cards missed, particularly the battalion number. The originals of these are still at TNA (in series WO 329), and are also available through some of the online genealogy service providers, such as Ancestry and Naval & Military Archive.

These sources should give you the basics you need to go forward with confidence that the person you are looking for, and the records you subsequently find, are the correct ones for your ancestor. More advice and guidance will be given later on where to go from here.

SUPPORTING GALLIPOLI

In addition to being the location of the ever crucial Suez Canal, Egypt's main role through 1915 was as the base of the Mediterranean Expeditionary Force (MEF), which was fighting on the Gallipoli Peninsula, trying to open the straits of the Dardanelles.

The majority of the forces in Egypt at this time were dedicated to the MEF. By July 1915, there were 81,000 soldiers (as well as 36,000 horses and 17,000 mules) in Egypt, of whom just 25,000 were actually assigned to the defence of the country. Another 15,000 men were Australians and New Zealanders ('Anzacs') still under training before being sent to Gallipoli, and 30,000 were logistical and support staff administering the MEF and its supply chain. The remaining 11,000 were sick and wounded who had been evacuated from Gallipoli and were now in Egyptian hospitals or convalescent homes.

The men waiting to go to Gallipoli lived either in the small permanent garrison buildings or, more likely, in large tented encampments near the big cities. Among other camps were Chatby Camp, on the shore near Alexandria and used by the cavalry, while the Australians used Mena Camp next to the Great Pyramids at Giza and nearby Meadi Camp, and the New Zealanders used Zeitoun Camp, also near Cairo. The basic conditions of the camps, the proximity to the cities and the mix of boredom and anxiety of the men waiting to be sent into battle meant that many troops entered the cities. Many went peacefully, visiting the tourist sites and museums, while others used the opportunity to drink and get into trouble. Discipline could be a problem and the army had to expand their police forces to patrol the streets of Cairo and Alexandria.

The logistical train for supporting the troops in Gallipoli was long and complicated. While the advance base of the MEF was the port of Mudros on the island of Lemnos, space there was limited. Many of the ships that brought supplies from across the world, as well as the huge amounts of food and other material grown or produced within Egypt itself, were gathered in Egyptian ports. Here they were stored, sorted and loaded back onto ships for movement to Lemnos or directly to the Dardanelles. Even fresh water, in several massive tankers, was exported from Egypt to supply the MEF.

The many different logistical units in Egypt, some supporting Gallipoli and others the troops in the country itself, as well as the different training organisations and finally the garrison troops themselves present challenges when researching this area. Many support units sprang in or out of existence, or were renamed, regularly. There is evidence that even the officers commanding these units became confused as to who they reported to at times! At Port Said, for example, the units overseeing the port passed from the command of the Canal Defence Force, to the Force in Egypt, to the Levant Base, and finally to the Egyptian Expeditionary Force all in the space of one month in early 1916.

There was also a large number of depots for mounted troops and other units (such as artillery) who used horses. These animals had to be left behind as, in the close confines of the Gallipoli Peninsula, the usually mounted troops fought on foot. Small cadres of men would be left to care for the horses, and as such would have their work cut out for them in an endless round of feeding, watering, grooming, exercising and mucking-out.

The hospital system had to expand rapidly in the summer of 1915, to support the unexpectedly large numbers of troops wounded at Gallipoli, and later those succumbing to the extremely high rates of sickness. Initially, many troops were evacuated directly to Egypt, often in whatever shipping was available. Later, properly equipped hospital ships made regular runs to Mudros, where advanced hospitals were established. If a

The Heliopolis Palace Hotel in Cairo, after being converted into a hospital to cope with the wounded coming from Gallipoli.

man was likely to recover within four weeks, he was held at Mudros. If his recovery would take longer, he would be sent on to Egypt (where there were some 35,000 hospital beds by the end of 1915) or to Malta.

The sheers numbers of wounded coming out of Gallipoli threatened to overwhelm the system in the early weeks of the campaign. While the army expanded their medical services as quickly as possible, some of the large numbers of British civilians in Egypt also pitched in to do their bit. One army officer's wife, Lady Margherita Howard de Walden, recalled the scene on the quayside:

> Casualties absolutely poured in. They unloaded them on to the quays where vans and lorries picked them up. In the meantime some had an hour or several hours lying unattended with the blazing sun tearing their nerves. So many wounds had developed gangrene on the voyage over,

with a shortage of nurses and frequently no one at all to change the dressings. Here Mary's [Aubrey] mother-in-law Lady Carnarvon worked. She collected other women and sunshades and organised cups of hot tea to cool and refresh these unhappy men. She was tiny, and white-haired with a quiet manner: the heart of a lion and indomitable determination and very persevering. (Quoted in A. Powell, *Women in the war zone: Hospital Service in World War 1* (Stroud, The History Press, 2009), p. 209)

Mary Aubrey was the wife of a staff officer. Lady Carnarvon, whose husband would fund the discovery of Tutankhamen's Tomb after the war, had allowed the army to use their home in England – Highclere Castle, now better known as the set for the TV series *Downton Abbey* – as a hospital.

After the end of the Gallipoli campaign, most of the troops involved were withdrawn to Egypt for between three and six months, where they were rested, re-equipped and re-trained before most of them were sent to France. A few divisions remained in Egypt, and these became the basis of the Egyptian Expeditionary Force in April 1916.

Chapter 3

SOLDIERS' LIVES

The suffering of the troops on the Western Front is well known, with the mud, barbed wire and desolate wasteland being familiar shorthand images for summing up the horrors of that, and indeed every other, war. Those who served in the Middle East theatres faced different trials – sometimes the complete opposite of their colleagues in France. Almost every aspect of daily life had to be tailored to fit the special circumstances which the troops found themselves in.

Some wartime and post-war narratives of the campaigns in Egypt and Palestine played down the difficulties faced by the troops. After all, the tempo of operations for the EEF was fairly low for much of the war, with long periods of seeming inactivity, and casualties were correspondingly fairly light. The two major military disasters faced by the EEF were their defeats at the 1st and 2nd Battles of Gaza in the spring of 1917, where the casualties were 4,000 and 6,500 killed, wounded or missing respectively. Bad enough, especially if you were one of them, but a drop in the ocean compared with the scale of the losses on the Somme or at Ypres.

The sun and the sand could give the mistaken impression that life among the 'pyramids and fleshpots' of the mysterious East was an extended holiday. In truth every day could be a struggle to survive in what was for most men an alien environment. It is perhaps hard to fully grasp this today, but not only did the population of pre-First World War Britain not enjoy the opportunities and ease of modern travel that we do today, but they did not even have the access to the magazines and newspapers full of colour photographs that we have

British infantry inspecting passing Arabs.

now, let alone the vast array of television programmes and films showing the wonders of other lands. The world that the men of the EEF faced when they landed at Alexandria would be quite literally one that they had never seen before, and for which nothing could have prepared them. Letters and memoirs are often filled with biblical references or occasional comparisons to literature such as the *Arabian Nights*, because these were the only frames of popular reference that the soldier could use to describe his environment that the reader could have any hope of understanding.

One of the biggest and most immediate differences confronting anyone would be the heat. In summer, temperatures routinely exceed 30 °C (90 °F) in the day time, while the khamsin, a hot blast of wind that blows for days on end up from the Sahara, can send them soaring to over 50 °C (over 120 °F) for long periods. Many soldiers mention this wind (using a variety of spellings!), and record that nothing could be done except sweat it out. Yeomanry Sergeant S.F. Hatton recalled spending several days cooped up in a tent with his best friend during one khamsin: 'Our tempers became very ragged, and though we had hutted together for some weeks, this afternoon we could have murdered each other. Things got worse and worse, until it was difficult to keep one's sanity.' (S.F. Hatton, *The Yarn of a Yeoman* (Uckfield, Naval & Military Press Ltd, 1930), p. 95).

Sandstorms were another danger. Moving around in them was dangerous due to how easily men could lose their way and stumble off into the desert. These too could last hours or even days, and soldiers could only fasten their tents or bivouacs as best as possible and ride it out. Men with horses to care for would often try to cover the animal's head at least, to keep the worst of the sand off them, but this was always difficult. When a storm was raging, it could be impossible for men to get food or, more importantly, water until after it was over.

At nights the temperatures fell drastically, and troops nearer the coast could find mist and dew forming and freezing on their sleeping bodies. One way to deal with the temperatures at night was to dig a rectangular hole to lie in, several feet deep and with a tent or bivouac set up over the top. The heat would penetrate deep into the sand during the day, and by digging into these warmer strata the men could benefit from the residual heat to some extent. Anthony Bluett recalled:

Our blankets, of which we had two, together with a greatcoat, cardigan-waistcoat, and a cap-comforter or balaclava helmet, this last a very stout bulwark against the cold blast. The first business was to dig a shallow, coffin-shaped trench large enough to contain two; it was much better for two men to bivouac together, since by putting one blanket only to sleep on, we had three with which to cover ourselves, besides our greatcoats. Nobody took any clothes off, with the exception of boots and putties . . . The pillow universally used was a nosebag filled with the next day's feed, and very comfortable it was . . . Then with our cap-comforters on, and perhaps the spare shirt wrapped round the head, we were snug for the night. (Bluett, *A Gunner's Crusade*, pp. 72–5)

Likewise, come dawn when the deeper layers had cooled and the upper ones began to heat up again, the trenches could keep men cooler for a while at least.

Digging trenches could also be useful in another way when it came to camping. Obviously, only very limited furniture could be carried with a marching column (although some folding tables and chairs for the headquarters were usually possible). However, a 'mess' (consisting of a group of men who habitually ate and lived together) could be formed by digging a rectangular trench. The officers or men could sit around the edge with their feet dangling into the trench, so at least they would not have to eat while standing, squatting or sitting on the ground, while the platform in the middle created a table.

Just as little furniture could be carried, the tents that each unit used in garrison or at the start of campaigns soon gave way to crude shelters and bivouacs. The canvas of the tents was not very durable in that climate, and besides, the pack-animal space used to transport so many tents could be put to better use carrying water, food or ammunition. Each time a unit stopped, there would be a scramble to collect palm fronds, bushes or branches that could be fashioned into shelters. This presumed of course that the unit stopped near some form of vegetation, although it was fairly rare not to: after all, where there was vegetation, there was water. Whatever could be gathered would then be lashed together for a shelter, and each man would have his own precious, jealously guarded stash of pieces of string and rope or even bits of canvas. The next task would then to be to find enough wood to start a fire, and get a billy of water boiling to make tea.

Later in 1917 the troops went from fighting in the sweltering deserts to being high in the wind-swept Judean Mountains during the rainy season in a matter of days. Such extreme changes badly affected not only physical health, but also morale. In the boulder strewn and largely treeless mountains (they look very different today to how they did a hundred years ago) digging or building shelters, or finding enough wood for a fire, was much more difficult, just at a time when freezing temperatures and driving rain made them most necessary. Private Henry Pope of the 2/15th London Regiment (2nd Civil Service Rifles) recorded in his diary for 1917:

> Christmas Eve!! Raining hard. Pack up and marched to hills in support as attack by Turks expected. Awful night, perishing cold and soaked through once more. Spent half the night carrying Lewis gun equipment from one place to another. Christmas Day – spent day in 'prehistoric stone cabin' or rather an alcove in some rocks with bivouac sheet for roof. Stay all day propped up on a stone because floor was a lake. Pouring with rain all day. Rations – 3oz of bully and about two biscuits. What a Christmas dinner! Half starved and shivering with cold. (Quoted J. Knight, *The Civil Service Rifles in the Great War: 'All Bloody Gentlemen'* (Barnsley, Pen and Sword Military, 2005), p. 194)

Those same rains also created massive problems further down the hills towards the coast. As the rain falling on the Judean Mountains swept down towards the sea, it created great areas of marshland. This not only disrupted supply lines as animals and vehicles got bogged down, and flash-floods swept away bridges over wadis, but also caused untold suffering to the men and horses stationed there. Sergeant Garry Clunie of the Wellington Mounted Rifles records the typical conditions faced through most of December 1917 and January 1918:

> 8 December: Still raining cats and dogs. Mud everywhere about 6 inches deep except horse lines which are about 18 inches. Stand to this morning was great, we had to dig some of our gear out of the mud. Water and exercised horses this morning and afternoon. Heavy rifle fire last night. We will probably relieve our mates in trenches . . . My bivvy is getting very wet inside with coming in with muddy boots. Shifted horse lines today. (K. Clunie and R. Austin (eds), *From Gallipoli*

Officers' Mess of the Royal Sussex Yeomanry in Egypt.

to Palestine: The War Writings of Sergeant G. T. Clunie of the Wellington Mounted Rifles, 1914–1919 (McCrae, Australia, Slouch Hat Publications, 2009), p. 176)

Those troops who later descended into the Jordan Valley also suffered in new and varied ways, as the atmosphere could be stifling, and the many standing pools of water led to prolific mosquitoes and widespread malaria.

The climate could be a grave danger to mental stability in the desert, and flies rapidly became another. They got everywhere and covered everything, especially food. Some soldiers tried to brush them away before eating, others, in resignation, simply ate the flies as well. Gunner Anthony Bluett recalled their effect after the war: 'It is no light thing that sends a strong man into hysterics or drives one sobbing from his tent, to rush about the camp in a frenzy of wild rage. Yet the flies did this – and more.' (Bluett, *A Gunner's Crusade*, p. 31).

As well as flies, sand also got everywhere. Clothes became caked in it, making cloth hard and abrasive, and it got into food and water too. This made it not only unpleasant to eat or drink, but could also lead to problems with the stomach and intestines. Indeed, the heat, sand and the flies were not just a nuisance, but also a severe danger. Only around 10 per cent of British casualties in Egypt and Palestine were caused by enemy action. Heatstroke and sunstroke were common, and disease was rife. In 1917 and 1918 malaria ran amok throughout the army. Unsurprisingly, given the hygiene problems caused by desert life, other constant issues were dysentery and diarrhoea. Poor sanitation also led to serious difficulties with sores and ulcers, many of which became infected. These could be caused by accidentally knocking bare skin against hot metal or leather, or through friction with sand-encrusted parts of uniforms. Corporal Victor Godrich recalled:

> Every man in the fighting forces was covered in sceptic sores on their hands, faces and legs – all in bandages. My own hands did not properly heal until the cold weather in December . . . If one's hand was accidentally knocked against a saddle, a large piece of skin came off. The result was an open sore that would not heal. The swarms of flies settling on the sore did not improve matters, so we had to use bandages for self-preservation. (V. Godrich, *Mountains of Moab: The diary of a cavalryman with the Queen's Own Worcestershire Hussars, 1908–1919* (Dr John Godrich, 2011), p. 108)

Godrich also recalled a sick parade when the entire regiment turned out: 'The first line were "bad" cases, wrecks etc. The second line "fairly bad" and the rear rank "not so bad."' Only the worst cases would be evacuated to the rear to be treated in hospital. Most sores, and later milder cases of malaria, would be dealt with as much as possible by the Field Ambulances and Aid Stations attached to the battalions and brigades, as to evacuate everyone who suffered would leave the front line almost completely unmanned. (See Chapter 5, Casualties.)

As much as possible was done to improve the living and working conditions of the soldiers at the front, or even the rear areas in the desert. New troops coming into Egypt would spend a week or two in relatively comfortable camps in Egypt, learning the basics of desert survival and gradually acclimatising to the heat. Here they learnt the EEF's patterns of work: starting early in the morning, and then stopping again late morning to let the worst of the heat pass, before restarting in the afternoon and working well into the night. This way, as much work was done as possible in the cooler periods of the day, and over midday the troops could rest and take what shelter they could.

The EEF also adapted in other ways. A wire-road (essentially long rolls of rabbit-wire pegged to the sand) was laid across the Sinai Desert, giving the men firmer footing on the soft sand. Otherwise, they would sink to their ankles in the sand with every step, necessitating much more effort. A relaxed approach to uniforms was also adopted, with men allowed to cut the arms short on their tunics, wear lighter sports-shoes or local slippers when off duty, and even convert their trousers into shorts. The historian of the 5th Highland Light Infantry recalled:

> We were allowed a good deal of latitude in the matter of the tunic and a man might choose whether he would increase the warmth of his body by wearing it, or the load on his back by putting it in his pack . . . As damaged articles could not be quickly replaced, a ragged pack often added to the bizarre aspect of the British soldier, with his dew-whitened helmet, squashed out of all decent shape, shirt of varied hue rolled back from sunburnt chest and arms usually marked by a dirty grey bandage or two, drill shorts stained, blackened and often torn, bare knees, puttees and rather disreputable boots. (*5th Battalion Highland Light Infantry*, Glasgow, MacLehose, Jackson & Co., 1921, p. 122)

British Yeomen in a temporary shelter or bivouac, while on patrol in the desert.

Digging could be a particular trial in the soft, shifting sands of the Sinai Desert. At one point, Gunner Anthony Bluett and his unit were sent to establish a defensive post in the desert to protect the southern end of the Suez Canal. He would later recall:

> There followed days of unremitting toil . . . With bowed backs and blistered hands [we] shovelled up half the desert and put it down somewhere else; the other half we put into sandbags and made gun pits of them . . . Day by day the sun waxed stronger until work became a torture unspeakable and hardly to be borne. With the slightest exertion the perspiration ran in rivulets from face and finger-tips; clothes became saturated and clung like a glove to our dripping bodies; and if a man stood for a time in one place the sand around was sodden with his sweat. (Bluett, *A Gunner's Crusade*, p. 28)

While he captures the suffering such digging caused, he misses the sheer amount of effort that would go into digging a trench in these circumstances. Anyone who has dug a hole on a beach will know that a simple slit could not be dug, as in France, as the sand merely slides back in again. Instead, a hole several times the size of the finished article had to be dug first, and then solid walls or 'rivetts' built to hold the sand back:

> This meant six hours' digging almost every day for almost every man, divided into a morning and an afternoon shift. Now sand is admittedly nice stuff to dig in, you do not need a pick, and can fill your shovel without exertion. But to trench in sand is not the faintest use unless it is revetted. Our revetting material was matting on wooden frames, and these had to be anchored back on stakes driven in deep down, six feet clear of the parapet . . . so that that to produce a trench you had to take out six feet of sand extra on either side, hammer in your stakes and attach your anchoring wires to the matting and then fill in the whole again. Traverses had to be dug right out and then filled in again when the wall of matting was in position and secure. (*5th Battalion Highland Light Infantry*, p. 82)

As can be imagined, water became an overriding obsession with the EEF, both as a force and as individuals. A pipeline was constructed across the Sinai Desert, running from near Cairo all the way into Palestine, to keep the army supplied. By May 1917 the pipeline was pumping 2.7 million litres (600,000 gallons) of water out of Egypt every day. Local sources were also developed wherever possible, to a sometimes astonishing extent. By the end of 1917, large sets of wells had been established or exploited at Khan Yunis and Shellal, on the border with Palestine. Eventually, 450,000 litres (100,000 gallons) of water would be pumped from the former and over 900,000 litres (200,000 gallons) from the latter every single day. Many smaller wells, springs and cisterns were also utilised to keep units supplied, although regulations stated that such water had to be first treated with chlorine. While this undoubtedly made it safe, it did little for the taste.

Every man was supposed to receive 4.5 litres (1 gallon/8 pints) per day, although this ration was seldom fully met. Not all of this went straight to the man: five pints per day went to the cookhouse, for cooking and making tea. Both of these played a vital role in maintaining health and morale. Food was often bland, with lots of stews, but at least they contained fresh vegetables and plenty of liquids. In camp in Egypt, the food could be quite good. Lance Corporal R. Loudon of the 4th Royal Scots recorded his daily rations while at a training camp near Cairo:

> Our rations in camp were tea, bread, bacon (or two eggs), cheese and jam for breakfast; tea, bread, cheese and jam for lunch (at 1 p.m.), and stew, or beef cooked in soup, and potatoes for dinner (at 5 pm). There was a YMCA hut in camp where we could purchase a cup of tea, and various titbits, very cheaply. (R. Loudon, IWM 87/17/1)

However, in the field, and particularly during big battles, the army had to resort to the standard rations of tins of bully beef and hard biscuits, neither of which were at all suitable for desert use. In the heat, bully beef turned in a saline mush, while the biscuits were almost impossible to eat with a dry mouth. Sometimes attempts were made to supplement rations with locally sourced food. Dates were plentiful and popular, as were oranges later in Palestine, but both could have a detrimental effect on the stomach if too many were eaten.

The water sent to the cookhouse also had another, live-preserving purpose: the brewing of tea, although most men (or at least sections) also maintained their own equipment for a 'brew' when needed. Lieutenant Briscoe Moore of the New Zealand Mounted Rifles found that:

> The early morning hours of darkness are the most trying, for then vitality is at its lowest and fatigued bodies ache all over. Then comes the first lightening of the eastern sky, and the new day dawns with a cheering influence, which is increased as the next halt gives the opportunity for a hurried 'boil-up' of tea; after which things seem not so bad after all to the dust-smothered and unshaven warriors. (Lieutenant A.B. Moore, *The Mounted Rifleman in Sinai and Palestine* (Auckland, Whitcombe & Tombs Ltd, 1920), p. 83)

Of the remaining three pints, two were issued for drinking, usually before dawn and after dusk. This was of course a severe trial. The historian of the 5th Highland Light Infantry explains:

> A single water-bottle, once filled, is but a poor supply for a long day under the Egyptian sun. Marching over heavy sand in the hot hours, even when the haversack has replaced the pack, soon produces an unparalleled drought. Sweat runs into a man's eyes and drips from his chin. It runs down his arms and trickles from his fingers. It drenches his shirt and leaves great white streaks on his equipment. And while so much is running out, the desire to put something in grows and grows. The temptation to take a mouthful becomes well nigh irresistible, and once the bottle of sun-heated chlorine-flavoured water is put to the lips, it is almost impossible to put it down before its precious contents are gone. (*5th Battalion Highland Light Infantry*, p. 98)

In combat, the suffering of the men could be even worse, as not only did physical exertion increase, but also supply systems almost inevitably broke down.

The final pint was for hygiene. The men in the desert where every bit as vulnerable to parasites as their comrades in France, as Sergeant Hatton again recalls:

I cannot describe to an ordinary cleanly person the most revolting sensation that a fellow undergoes when first he discovers that he had become the prey of body-lice. I think I was more inclined to be sick at their appearance than at anything I saw or smelt during the whole War. After a time one got quite used to the little pests, and entered into the sport of the daily 'louse' with glee. (Hatton, *The Yarn of a Yeoman*, p. 74)

One useful trick denied to those on the Western Front was to lay infected clothes over an ant hill. The ants would swarm up and eat the lice and their eggs, and for a time at least (once the ants had been shaken off) some relief could be found.

This single pint could sometimes be assisted by using undrinkable water. In some areas of the Sinai, digging into the sand far enough could bring brackish water seeping up into the hole, which could then be used for a rudimentary bath. Divisions would frequently be rotated to allow them to spend short periods near the Mediterranean coast, where sea bathing was a popular pastime. At other times, troops simply had to make the most of what little they had. Lieutenant James Mackie of the 2/4th Somerset Light Infantry had served in India before his battalion was posted to Palestine, and so was no stranger to hot climates, but even so he found the lack of water trying:

We don't waste very much I can assure. We use about a pint every morning to wash, shave & clean our teeth in & then this water is used by our batmen to wash socks etc in before it is thrown away. We can't afford water to wash our plates in but sand makes a very good substitute & you can get them just as clean by rubbing them with sand as by washing them in water. As a matter of fact they don't want much cleaning for we clean them fairly well with bread before we finish our meals for even a drop of gravy is too valuable to waste. (J.H.F. Mackie (ed.), *Answering the Call: Letters from the Somerset Light Infantry, 1914–1919* (Eggleston, Raby Books, 2002), p. 293)

Gunner Anthony Bluett perhaps sums up the EEF soldier's attitude to water in all of its uses: 'You, who dwell in temperate climes, with water – hot and cold – at a hand's turn, will perhaps accuse me of labouring the point. I cannot help it; no words of mine can express what it meant to have that clean feeling for just an hour or two. It was ineffable luxury; it helped us to endure.' (Bluett, *A Gunner's Crusade*, p. 29)

WILDLIFE

The men of the EEF found animals and other wildlife to be both their friends and their enemies. Some such relationships were obvious – the men who worked with horses mostly developed deep and warm relationships with them – while the constant swarms of flies could drive even the mildest man into a mad frenzy. Sometimes animals elicited both extremes of emotion. Camels, for example, were hated for their bad tempers and stubborn nature, and even feared for their occasional violence. But they were also loved by their handlers (after a time) for being tough and resilient, and because of the natural bond that grows up between any animals and their owners. Whichever animal they had, the men who used horses or camels also had a considerable burden added to them in caring for their beasts, which could take several hours a day.

Apart from the animals that were employed by the army officially, many others were co-opted for a variety of uses by soldiers. Some of these experiments were less than successful; many tried to vary their rations while stationed in Egypt by eating the flamingos that lived around the Suez Canal. Captain (and Medical Officer) Oskar Teichman discovered that they were 'of no use as food' (Captain O. Teichman, DSO MC, *The diary of a Yeomanry M.O.* (London, T. Fisher Unwin Ltd, 1921), p. 47). In fact, according to Sergeant Hatton, flamingo meat would turn green on being cooked and 'was as tough as old boots, and of a similar flavour' (Hatton, *The Yarn of a Yeoman*, p. 96).

Yeomen taking care of their horses, which could take hours of extra work every day.

Chameleons proved more useful, as they could be put on leashes and allowed to sit on branches tied to tent poles, where they would work on decreasing the fly population. Soldiers quickly learned to check their boots, bedrolls and other equipment for scorpions, centipedes and spiders each morning, which could deliver a nasty sting or bite. They could also be captured and used to divert bored soldiers by being put into makeshift rings in order to fight each other, on which bouts considerable betting could take place. For the more patient (and army life, particularly in a desert, did encourage patience), tortoise racing was popular:

Tortoise racing was a slow business, but eminently sporting, because the tortoise is so splendidly unreliable. On one occasion one of the competitors in a big sweepstake was discovered to consist of a shell only – the tortoise who had once dwelt therein having died and turned to dust. In consideration of this it was given a start of six inches, but long odds were offered against it. However, at the end of the time limit – eight minutes – no competitor had moved at all, so that the tortoiseless one was adjudged the winner amid great applause. ('5th Highland Light Infantry', pp. 113–14)

More traditional sports were followed with the hunting of pi-dogs and jackals. Several units had their own, albeit small, hunting packs. The Royal Gloucestershire Hussars for example had managed to bring two hounds out with them from England, named Tripe and Onions.

Snakes were a big problem in the Judean Mountains. Many were extremely poisonous, and the casualty rate was getting unacceptably high (three out of four bitten soldiers were dying according to Teichman). HQ put out word that they wanted specimens, specifically snakes' skulls and spinal cords, to use in developing anti-venoms. Teichman recalled:

I was called down to the horse lines, where I found a large black snake, some ten feet long, pinned down with two swords. One of our officers who had served in the Sudan and South Africa identified the snake as a very poisonous one known as the Black Mamba . . . As the head and some two feet of the snake were free of the first sword, we managed to catch the former with some wire-nippers and transfix it also with another sword. Eventually the whole snake was pinned out on the grass with some six swords piercing its body, but not interfering with the spinal cord . . . Sending for a bottle of chloroform, we solemnly anaesthetized our patient, eventually giving it a considerable overdose and pouring an ounce into its mouth, which was held open by means of wire-nippers. The snake was now inert, and was rolled up in a large native fig-basket ready for removal . . . to Headquarters at Jerusalem. An hour later a horrified orderly met me, saying that the snake had come to life again! On-going down to the medical tent we found that this was true, and that the snake was slowly emerging from the basket, apparently none the worse for its experience. One felt inclined not to obey the instructions this time, but to cut off its head with a convenient spade. However . . . we went through the same performance, but after the snake had been pinned down I determined to take no chances, and with a couple of farriers holding the snake's head with their pincers, I emptied one pound of Burgoyne's best army chloroform into the reptile's mouth; he didn't seem to like the drink, but was compelled to swallow it, and appeared to be stone dead when the bottle was empty. However, this time we were not going to give him time to come to life; he was packed into his fig-basket, which was securely tied up with ropes and was placed on the back of a dispatch rider's motor-cycle, which dashed off up the Latron road to Jerusalem . . . We often wondered what happened to our snake, and whether he ever came to life again, but thought it wiser not to investigate the matter any further. (Teichman, 'Diary of a Yeomanry MO', pp. 249–50)

Wildlife did not just mean animals. The flora of Palestine could be quite spectacular, and even today it is well worth a trip to the Sea of Galilee in the autumn to see the magnificent blooms. General Allenby, as well as being a keen angler and bird-watcher, was interested in flowers, and Lieutenant Colonel G.E. Badcock, one of his logistical staff, recalled: 'The Chief was a great lover of flowers, and many a time motoring along the Ludd–Jerusalem or Latrun–Ram Allah roads you might see him on the hill-sides with his arms full of those wonderful flowers that grew in such profusion in the months of March and April in Palestine.' (Lieutenant Colonel G.E. Badcock, *A history of the Transport Services of the Egyptian Expeditionary Force, 1916–1917–1918* (London, Hugh Rees Limited, 1925), p. 310).

Chapter 4

RESEARCHING BRITISH AND DOMINION SOLDIERS

In the summer of 1940, the Battle of Britain raged in the skies over London. On 7 September the Germans changed their strategy, and began a campaign of almost continual bombing of London and the other major cities which would last six months. Among the many tragedies on that first day of what became the Blitz was the bombing of the War Office Repository on Arndale Street, which was burned out that night. Huge amounts of First World War records were lost, including service records and card indexes for nurses and chaplains, courts martial proceedings, casualty records, card indexes and citations for many honours and awards, and documents relating to the EEF, the Imperial Camel Corps and the Zionist Mule Corps (both of which served in Egypt and Palestine).

The most well-known loss, and so big that estimates vary as to even how large, was the destruction of Records of Service for both officers and other ranks. Anything from 4 to 5.25 million of the 6.5 million Records of Service were destroyed, or anything from 60–80 per cent. One of the reasons why estimates vary is that many partial records were salvaged and painstakingly pieced back together (what are now known as the 'Burnt Records', which we will discuss later), while others were filed elsewhere. The main point here is that the bulk of the most comprehensive records on each individual were lost.

The Record of Service is just that: a record of the individual's enlistment, units and postings or transfers between them, promotions, disciplinary record, medical record and discharge.

A classic view! These types of photos were a popular souvenir for members of the EEF.

Some of those for men who were killed also include the forms that the families had to fill in before receiving their bronze Memorial Plaque and scroll, with details of the family as well as on the individual.

Much of the Record is based on different lists of dates, and it can help you to understand the Record if you use the different elements to compile a single chronology of your relative's service. This will give you the basic framework, but it is by no means a complete 'blow-by-blow' account of their service. For example, if the person stays with the same unit for two years, and did not get wounded, promoted, awarded a medal or do anything particularly bad in that period, you may not find anything at all for that time. You will not get a note of every time that unit moved, or what actions they took part in. You certainly will not get anything near a day-by-day list of movements and activities. This sort of information comes from the unit War Diary, which we will discuss later.

We will look at Records of Service first, and then at ways that you can work around any missing records and build a picture from other extant records.

OFFICERS' RECORDS OF SERVICE

Files on about 85 per cent of officers are held at TNA, but it is fair to say that they are a shadow of their former selves. The Records that still exist are 'supplementary' or 'correspondence' or 'miscellaneous' files (different sources used different terms for them), containing paperwork weeded out of the main Records which were unfortunately lost in 1940. Therefore, the contents of the files varies considerably. Some include a copy of the actual Record of Service (sheet of dates etc.), but most only contain peripheral information, although this can be invaluable by itself.

Some files will contain paperwork from when the individual was first commissioned. If they came up through the ranks – i.e. served as a common soldier before either applying or being recommended for a commission – this may include documents relating to their previous service, original enlistment and perhaps a recommendation or reference from their previous commanding officer. If they applied to join the army as an officer, their original application form (Army Form MT393A) may be included, which like any job application form will include basic biographical details.

Other paperwork will relate to the end of their service. Discharge and pension papers may be there, including post-war correspondence. If the officer was killed, there may be correspondence with his family, and paperwork relating to their personal effects, the settling of their accounts, any wills, or applications for widow's pensions. If the officer was posted as missing, there may be appeals from the family for more information as well.

The officers' Records of Service are held in two series at TNA:

- WO 339: This series contains the files of Regular army and Emergency Reserve officers, and is arranged in Long Number order. Officers did not have service numbers as such, but each was given a file referenced by a unique Long Number. The Long Number for your officer can be found by looking in Series WO 338, which contains an alphabetical list of officers and their numbers.

- WO 374: This series contains the files of officers who served in the TF or had temporary commissions. These were originally two separate series, known as the 'Vowel Series' after the prefixes given to temporary commissions, and the '9 Series' after the prefix given to the numbers allocated to TF officers. The two series were merged by the Ministry of Defence before release, and placed in alphabetical order. However, as with any alphabetical records mistakes do occur so it is always worth checking a few records either side of where your relative should be, while there is also a collection of stray files that came out of order and are now gathered at the end of the series.

In both of the above series the provisos are that if the officer stayed in the army after 1922, or if they re-joined the army during the Second World War, their records are still held by the Ministry of Defence, and can be applied for through this site: https://www. gov.uk/guidance/requests-for-personal-data-and-service-records. All of the other officer's Records of Service are available at or through TNA, and the index can also be searched through Find My Past.

SOLDIERS' RECORDS OF SERVICE

As mentioned already, the Records of Service for other ranks are much rarer than those for officers. The contents of the Records for other ranks is also as varied and as inconsistent as in those for officers. Again, several different types of record may be in the file, either from separate or from overlapping timeframes, and it can be an extremely useful exercise to compile your own chronological list of events from them.

Some Records will include the soldier's attestation document, which he filled in with his basic biographical details, including address and occupation, when he joined the army. If it survives, Army Form B103 'Casualty Form – Active Service' can be a goldmine of information. It gives far more than just sickness or wounds, but also includes all of the man's promotions, transfers, postings and disciplinary information. This form, even more so than the others, can be a barely comprehensible muddle of jargon and abbreviations, but thankfully the genealogist has never had better sources of assistance on hand to help. Websites such as The Long Long Trail (www.long longtrail.co.uk) and Great War (www.greatwar.co.uk) have reams of advice and lists of abbreviations for you to search. If you really become stuck, an appeal on the Great War Forum (http://1914-1918.invasion zone.com) seldom fails to find some expert who can help.

The Record will also cover, one way or another, the end of the soldier's service, with the dates and reasons for death or discharge. There may also be additional correspondence about pensions, wills, personal effects or other letters from the soldier or his next of kin.

If your relative stayed in the army after 1920, or reenlisted during the Second World War, their record will still be with the Ministry of Defence, and you can apply for access through the same website given for officer's Records, above.

The surviving Records of Service are held by TNA, under two references:

- WO 363: These are the so-called 'Burnt Records'. They are the fragments rescued from the 1940 fire that have been pieced back together and microfilmed, and more recently digitised.
- WO 364: The 'Unburnt Records'. These are Records of Service that were filed or in use elsewhere when the War Office Repository was bombed, and so are complete and undamaged. They are sometimes also known as the 'Pension Records' because many had been in use with the files of soldiers who had claimed pensions due to wounds or injuries received during their service.

A Signal Section with the tools of their trade – signalling flags and heliographs (mirrors).

Incidentally, the Records of officers and men who served with the Household Cavalry and the Guards Regiments were kept separately and survive largely intact. None of these units served in Egypt or Palestine, but there may have been a few men who did and then transferred to the Household Cavalry or the Guards later. These records are held by the Household Cavalry Museum and the respective Guards Regiments.

If your ancestor had also served before the First World War, for example, as one of the volunteers for the Boer War, it is also worth searching WO 97, which contains earlier records and may record some details on the later reenlistment.

The Records that are at TNA are obviously accessible at Kew, and through Ancestry and Find My Past. The Records were sifted into alphabetical order before being microfilmed and the usual caveats apply about searching either side of where you expect your relative to be, and checking the miscellaneous reels at the end of the series which includes those that for whatever reason were missed out from their proper place.

They are also available on both Ancestry and Find My Past. It is worth noting that Find My Past compiled their own indexes for WO 363 and WO 364, which they say has turned up a considerably larger number of names than are on TNA's (and thus Ancestry's) indexes, and this is because they include names of spouse, children etc. Find My Past has also compiled all of their British Army Records of Service from 1760 to 1920 into a single series, so when using their search engine it is important to put WO 363 and WO 364 into the 'Series' search field.

NO RECORD OF SERVICE?

If your ancestor is one of the many whose Record of Service was either destroyed or is incomplete, do not despair: there are other avenues that you can explore. Many of them deal with how their service ended, with either death or discharge, but others can provide insights into their actual service too.

GALLANTRY MEDALS AND AWARDS

A range of medals and awards could be granted for bravery or other distinguished service. Some would be 'immediate' awards, granted 'in the field' for a specific action. Others would be non-immediate, for general or consistent conduct and awarded in one of the bi-annual lists – the New Year's Honours List and the King's Birthday List (published in June).

Gallantry awards had their own hierarchy. At the top of course was the Victoria Cross (VC), still Britain's highest award for bravery, and details on the men who won the VC in Egypt and Palestine can be found in Gerald Gliddon's *VCs of the First World War: The Sideshows* (Stroud, Sutton Publishing, Sutton Publishing, 2005). Apart from the obvious mistake of considering Egypt and Palestine 'sideshows', this is an excellent book.

The VC could be awarded to anyone regardless of rank, but the other four main gallantry awards were segregated. The Distinguished

Service Order (DSO) was for officers of all services, and generally awarded to Majors and above, although awards to lower ranks were not unknown. This award covered that nebulous concept 'leadership' as well as bravery per se, and could be awarded for an officer's performance in commanding his unit in action. Next came the Military Cross (MC), which was created in 1914 to reward bravery in the field by officers of the rank of Captain and below, and for Warrant Officers. The RN equivalent of the MC was the Distinguished Service Cross (DSC) for Officers below the rank of Lieutenant Commander and Warrant Officers, while when the RAF was formed in 1918 they created the Distinguished Flying Cross (DFC) for their own use.

For other ranks, there was the Distinguished Conduct Medal (DCM), the oldest bravery medal in the British Army (beating the VC by just over a year). So many were awarded in the first eighteen months of the First World War that in March 1916 the Military Medal (MM) was created as a slightly lower level award, to reflect the perceived levels of gallantry involved in each act. The RN meanwhile had the Distinguished Service Medal (DSM), while in 1918 the new RAF created the Distinguished Flying Medal (DFM), again both for other ranks.

In each of the above cases, the medal could be awarded to a man more than once. In these circumstances, rather than a separate medal being issued, a 'Bar' was awarded to the existing one. This was, literally, a small bar of metal that was fixed to the ribbon of the medal. There was no limit on how many Bars could be awarded for each medal. Soldiers would only wear their full medals on specific official occasions, but at other times would have a small rectangular piece of the medal's ribbon fixed to their tunic just above the left breast pocket. If these were being worn, the Bar was denoted by a small rosette on the appropriate ribbon.

Separate to these awards was a Mention in Despatches (MiD, although they can also appear on Medal Index Cards as 'EM' or 'EMB'). These were simply that – a sign that an officer or a soldier had performed some act that had been seen as worthy of mention in the commanding general's official despatch back to London (i.e. his official report on a particular action or campaign). This could be a minor act of bravery, or it could be any other manner of contribution. For example, logistics or administrative staff might get a mention for keeping the supplies flowing and the army fed under particularly difficult conditions, or an engineer for recommending or implementing a solution to a particular problem. Frustratingly, in almost every case, the general writing the despatch would simply list the names of those whose contributions he wished to draw attention to, without any explanation of why. They were awarded regardless of rank, and came with a letter of thanks from the King and a small bronze oak leaf that would be fixed to the ribbon of the Victory Medal. Just over 2 per cent of those who served were Mentioned at some point.

Medals can be surprisingly difficult to research because all the paperwork was destroyed in 1940. All awards appeared in the *London Gazette*, the government's official newspaper, which can be searched on its website: www.thegazette.co.uk. Unfortunately, it is not the easiest search engine to use, but the *Gazette* will give you confirmation of the name, rank, number (for other ranks) and unit of the individual, as well as the date of the award. Particularly at times of heavy action, the lists in the *Gazette* could run days or weeks behind the actual dates of award. For the higher level awards, the citation for the award will also appear. A complete set of the wartime *Gazettes* is also available on DVD-ROM from Naval & Military Press.

The citation is the official statement saying why someone was receiving that particular award. Unfortunately, for most awards they are very hard, if not impossible, to find. Mentions in Despatches have already been discussed, and citations for the 115,000 or so Military Medals awarded were lost in the 1940 fire, although a list of recipients is available on The Genealogist. DCMs on the other hand are well documented, with the citations on both Ancestry and Find My Past. Other citations remain in files at TNA, and you should consult their guide on this subject, as it is unfortunately far too complicated to include here.

If no citations exist, it is worth checking both the unit and the brigade War Diaries. The unit War Diary will at the very least show what was happening that day, and may give some indication of why an award was made, for example, in relation to a particular action. It is relatively unlikely that it will go into any great detail, but it will at least give an idea of what was going on. Very occasionally they will include a copy (or a draft) of the original recommendation, usually as an appendix to the monthly diary. Likewise, brigade War Diaries will give an idea of where a unit was and what sort of activities they were involved in, and also, because recommendations had to be endorsed by the brigade commander, there is an outside chance that a copy was kept on file.

Other sources worth looking at include regimental histories – which again will tell you what was happening to that unit on that day, and may even mention an individual's bravery – and local newspapers, which often ran stories on local lads who received awards.

SILVER WAR BADGE

The Silver War Badge (SWB) was introduced by the government for use by men who had been honourably discharged from the army, for example, because of wounds or sickness. It was not uncommon for seemingly able-bodied men to be harassed in the street in the UK for not being in uniform or being at the front. In September 1916 the SWB was introduced for veterans to wear as a visible mark that they had 'done their bit'. Any man who had been honourably discharged since the start of the war could apply for one, and the badges that were issued were numbered and recorded in a register. In all, over 880,000 were issued.

The badge itself was circular and made of silver. The King's cipher and a crown were in the centre, surrounded by a rim containing the words 'For King and Empire' and 'Services Rendered', while the number is on the back.

Incidentally, these badges should not be confused with the 'Imperial Service' badge used by the TF, which was rectangular with those words on it and the King's crown above. Men of the TF could not be compelled to serve overseas, but many volunteered to do so. Those men would be issued the Imperial Service badge as a mark of that commitment before they were actually sent, and so again could avoid possible accusations of cowardice. 'On War Service' badges were also issued to personnel involved in reserved occupations. Several different designs were used, some issued by the government and others by individual employers. Not only would these protect wearers from scorn, but some (such as for munitions shift-workers) granted priority boarding on public transport, along with cheaper fares.

The serial numbers on the SWB can be used to trace an entry in the registers, which are available as images of the actual entry through Ancestry, or as transcripts through Find My Past or Naval & Military Archive, or in their entirety on a CD-ROM from the Naval & Military Press. The register will give the man's name, rank, service number (except for officers), unit, dates of enlistment and discharge, and the reason for discharge, although this is likely to simply be 'sick' or 'wounds'. In around a third of cases the age of the recipient is also given. If no Record of Service exists for your relative, the SWB could be the only source for some of this information.

ABSENT VOTERS LISTS
These may well be familiar to genealogists already. For the General Election of 1918, soldiers aged 21 and over were registered on Absent Voters lists, which recorded their names, usually their service numbers, sometimes their unit and their home address. Not all eligible soldiers were registered, and not all Lists survive. Those that do are usually held in local records offices around the country, although some are at the British Library, and some are available through the various online genealogical services. There is a comprehensive list of the surviving records on The Long Long Trail (www.1914-1918.net).

COURTS MARTIAL

Many soldiers committed some offence or other during their time in uniform. Most of these were fairly minor and to do with appearance, condition of kit, being late for duty or such like. These would be dealt with at unit level, with small-scale stoppages of pay, extra duty or short periods confined to barracks ('CB'). For more serious crimes a man could choose whether to be tried by his Commanding Officer, or by a Regimental or a District Court Martial (for Corporals and above, it had to be a District Court Martial). The process with the CO was more arbitrary, and with fixed limits of up to twenty-eight days each of either Field Punishment, detention or stoppages of pay, or for drunkenness a fine of up to 10s. The full range of lesser punishments was also available. A Regimental Court Martial could extend punishments up to forty-two days, or a District Court Martial could also reduce NCOs to the ranks, order the offender to be discharged or even sentence them to penal servitude. For the highest level crimes – rape, murder, cowardice, desertion, sleeping on sentry duty, striking a superior officer, mutiny and a host of others – the soldier would be brought before a General Court Martial, which had the power of passing the death sentence, among other lesser punishments.

Such serious crimes seem to have been less frequent in Egypt and Palestine, although it is hard to be exact due to the lack of surviving records. Just three men were 'shot at dawn' in Egypt or Palestine: two for murder and the other for brutally assaulting an NCO with a club while already serving a prison term. Perhaps the environment in which the EEF operated worked in their favour. After all, where would deserters run to in the desert, or to even go 'absent without leave' to for long periods. Likewise, the general tempo of operations was lower than in France, so the stresses on the men in this respect were less. A major factor was that the EEF seems to have adopted a rather less formal and practical approach to discipline, more suitable to their circumstances and perhaps based on the fact that the units of the EEF were all either from the TF or formed from wartime enlistees. These 'citizen soldiers' had a somewhat more laid back approach to discipline to that of the regular army.

Field Punishment, which came in two forms, must have been a particularly harsh experience in Egypt and Palestine. Field Punishment No. 1 involved being shackled to an item – a fixed post or a wagon wheel for example – for 2 hours out of every 24, for three days in every four, for up to twenty-one days. While it is likely that such punishments would not have been held during the worst of the heat of the day, it still must have been a deeply uncomfortable experience. Under Field Punishment No. 2, the offender was shackled but not to a fixed point.

Very few records of these punishments still exist, although some records survive at TNA, particularly in WO 90, but also in WO 71, WO 93 and WO 213. However, punishments would be noted on the Records of Service, and more serious ones may come up in pension applications.

WILLS

Every serviceman was encouraged to write a will, and indeed a sample was included in their pay books. Some soldiers' wills are filed at the UK Probate Office just like anyone else's. These can be searched for in the usual way, at www.gov.uk/probate -search, and copies ordered for a small fee.

If the wills were put into force, or 'proved', due to the death of the soldier, then they would be announced in the National Probate Calendar, albeit up to six months after the date of death. These can be searched on Ancestry.

The National Archives of Scotland has released around 26,000 soldier's wills online, which can be searched at www.scotlands people.gov.uk.

The wills of Irish soldiers can be found through the National Archives of Ireland website at www.soldierswills.nationalarchives.ie.

SOLDIERS' EFFECTS RECORDS

These ledgers recorded the final accounts of soldiers who had been killed. Once their pay had been tallied, and arrears added in and their reductions removed, and the standard small gratuity awarded, the remaining monies would be paid out to their next of kin. The ledgers record this final reckoning, starting with the name, rank, number and unit of the soldier, and the date and place of death. On the accounting side, the amounts involved are given, with the details of who they were paid to. This would be the next of kin – widow if applicable, father if the soldier was unmarried and then through a hierarchy of other relatives if their father had already died: their mother, and then siblings, and so on. The names of these recipients are given.

All of the Soldiers' Effects Records from 1901 to 1960 are held by the National Army Museum, and can be accessed through them at www.nam.ac.uk. The Records from 1901 to 1929 are also available through Ancestry.

PENSION RECORDS

There are several types of pensions. Most obvious are those for soldiers who were unable to continue their service due to wounds or sickness, who would be assessed for and usually receive a pension, if only for a short period. Less obvious are those that were claimed after a man had been discharged at the end of his service in the usual way. As part of the demobilisation, or 'demob', process, every man was given a medical examination and asked to declare any wounds or previous illness. If the wounds or illness had debilitated the man, he could be granted a pension, again even if just for a short period. Victor Godrich, for example, on being discharged: 'Informed [the Medical Officer] that I had suffered from enteric fever and malaria to which I was still prone. This was entered in my medical record and much to my surprise I was awarded a disability pension of 10/- weekly which I enjoyed for 2 years.' (Godrich, *Mountains of Moab*, p. 196).

The two diseases mentioned by Victor were common ailments in the EEF, and this story must have been played out many times as the veterans returned home. These men could, in later life, claim a pension if, for example, they were unable to work due to recurring sickness or old wounds picked up during their service.

The widows and dependants of soldiers who had been killed could also claim a pension. This would be calculated in part, where relevant, on the number of children involved, and a schedule would be drawn up that would steadily decrease the allowance as each child reached the age of 16.

Estimates vary as to how many pension records there are still surviving at TNA, although everyone agrees that it is only a few per cent of those pensions granted. They are spread across a bewildering array of series and files, and it is recommended that you read TNA's own guide to the pension records before embarking on a search, not least because of the way the files are organised. Some are indexed by name, but many of them are in date order. In brief, the records still held are:

- WO 364: Known as the 'Unburnt Files', these roughly 750,000 records have been discussed before. Most of these Records of Service had been withdrawn from the main run of records (destroyed in 1940) for use in pension-related work.
- PIN 26: A representative selection of about 22,000 files on those awarded or refused pensions from 1920.
- PIN 82: A representative selection of files on claims by widows and dependants, 1910–32.
- PMG 4: Records relating to officers going on half-pay (i.e. retiring from active service), 1737–1921.
- PMG 9: Records relating to pensions for wounds, 1814–1921.
- PMG 42: Records relating to temporary retired pay and gratuities to officers and nurses, 1917–20.
- PMG 43: Records on special grants and allowances to officers' widows and dependants, 1916–20.
- PMG 44: Records relating to pensions to officers' widows and dependents, 1916–20.
- PMG 45: Records relating to pensions for officers' widows, 1917–19.

- PMG 46: Records relating to allowances for the children of officers killed, 1916–20.
- PMG 47: Records relating to interim pensions for relatives of officers posted as missing, 1915–20.

WO records are of course those of the War Office; less well known, PIN are those of the Ministry of Pensions and National Insurance, and PMG of the Paymaster General's Office.

Also, series PT6 at the National Archives of Scotland deals with pensions to Scottish soldiers and next of kin.

PENSION CARDS

Given how jumbled and incomplete the records mentioned above are, it seems incredible that in 2011 the Ministry of Defence released some 6.5 million First World War pension cards, and that TNA declined to take them. Thankfully, the WFA stepped in and secured the survival of this invaluable resource. It includes:

- Nearly 1 million cards on other ranks who had been killed.
- Over 1 million cards on next of kin and dependants of other ranks who had been killed.
- Over 2.5 million cards on other ranks who requested and either received or were declined a pension.
- 150,000 cards on officers who survived or the widows of those who were killed.
- 5,000 cards relating to men who served in the Merchant Navy.

Each card records the basic details of service of the individual – name, rank, number, regiment and date of death or discharge. If applicable, the names, addresses and dates of birth of the dependants are also given, with, in the case of the children, a schedule showing when each would reach the age of 16. The amounts awarded are recorded, along with the schedule of how they would change over time or come to an end. And these were not just snapshot records, either: they were kept up to date as people moved or their wounds or sickness improved or got worse.

There are also about 15,000 ledgers, each of which deals with about 100 individuals who were in receipt of pensions. The ledgers were kept by type (i.e. separate sets for each service, for widows, for dependants etc.), and were kept regionally, presumably relating to the different regional assessment boards. Not all have survived.

Obviously, this collection, not available through the usual online genealogy sources, can provide invaluable information. The WFA are planning to digitise the complete set in the long run, but for the time being the cards can be accessed (for a fee) via the WFA. You will need to provide as much detail as possible, and there are forms and details on payment on their website at www.westernfrontassociation.com.

Incidentally, despite its name, the WFA is dedicated to all theatres and aspects of the First World War, including the campaigns in Egypt and Palestine. Members receive three copies each of the WFA's two magazines every year, and also details on their local branches, which run (usually monthly) talks and events.

ROLLS OF HONOUR

There is an astonishing range of Rolls of Honour available to First World War researchers, although it has to be said that the level of detail in many of them is quite scant, and the quality varies greatly.

The most comprehensive Roll of service personnel killed during the First World War is found on the CWGC website at www.cwgc. org/find-war-dead.aspx. This records the name, rank, unit, service number and date of death, as well as the exact location of where they are buried (i.e. plot, row and grave as well as the cemetery), if they have a known grave. If they do not have a known grave, anyone killed in Egypt, Palestine or Syria will be recorded on the Jerusalem Memorial to the missing. This wall of names runs across the back of the Jerusalem War Cemetery on Mount Scopus, where it commands striking views across the city. Other details can also be recorded by CWGC, such as the name and address of the next of kin or awards and medals held by the individual. Recently, the CWGC has started adding extra documents to each entry, including the page from the relevant Cemetery Register and details on the 'concentration' of the body (i.e. moving them from a field grave to an established cemetery) where applicable. Details of the small inscription that each family was allowed to have engraved in the foot of the headstone (free up to a certain number of letters) can also be found.

While the CWGC's site does not show photographs of the individual grave, the War Graves Photographic Project does. This is an on-going, non-profit-making and volunteer organisation dedicated to taking a photograph of every official and unofficial grave or memorial for every member of the British armed services from 1914 onwards around the world. Ambitious as it is, at the time of writing they have images of some 1.8 million graves and memorials. Low-resolution photographs can be seen on the website, or prints can be ordered for a small administrative fee. See www.twgpp.org for more details.

The next most comprehensive Rolls are the 'Soldiers Died in the Great War' and 'Officers Died in the Great War' lists produced by HMSO in 1921, and which record 662,000 men and 41,000 officers respectively. These only cover the army, and are produced in volumes specific to particular regiments or corps. They give the basic details of each man – name, rank, number, unit – as well as the date and cause of death, the theatre where they were killed and sometimes details on dates of birth and places of enlistment and residence. They have been digitised by the Naval & Military Press, and are available in their entirety on a CD-ROM, or they are also searchable through Ancestry and Find My Past.

A number of 'subscription' Rolls were published during and just after the war, where families could subscribe to have their relative's details included. The level of detail in these is not always very high, and they were not checked for accuracy, but they can still be very useful.

The National Roll of the Great War was intended to cover the whole country by regions, but only a few volumes were produced before the enterprise went bust. In all, about 10 per cent of the country is covered, giving details (including addresses) of other ranks who had been killed. Copies are accessible through various libraries, or through Ancestry and Naval & Military Archive.

'A Biographical Record of His Majesty's Military and Aerial Forces who Fell in the Great War' was started by the 9th Marquis of Ruvigny and Raineval, himself a keen genealogist, and is more commonly known for obvious reasons as De Ruvigny's Roll of Honour. It eventually ran to 5 volumes, recording 26,000 casualties of all ranks and including about 7,000 photographs. Again the details were provided by the family and are therefore unverified, and can run from very basic details through to an entire biography complete with extracts from letters. The entries are generally from the earlier part of the war, as De Ruvigny embarked on his project before the full scale of the losses became apparent, swamping his system. Copies can be accessed through various libraries (including the online digital library www.archive.org) or through Ancestry, Find My Past and Naval & Military Archive.

A different type of Roll is Ireland's Memorial Records, which was produced by the Committee of the Irish National War Memorial in 8 volumes, recording some 49,000 men and women. This is a comprehensive list of all of those lost who were either born in Ireland, resident in Ireland at the time of enlistment or who served in Irish regiments. It gives their name, rank, number, unit, date, cause and place of death, and their birthplace. It can be accessed through Find My Past and Ancestry.

There are also a staggering number of Rolls based on everything from home towns to schools and universities to places of work. Many towns and organisations created their own Rolls in the years just after the war, and there has been a steady stream of such Rolls being produced ever since, with a natural flurry over the period of the centenary commemorations. Some of these are based on the announcements or obituaries in local newspapers, which are also a good source in and of themselves, and which can usually be found in local libraries or county archives, although they can also be accessed through the British Library's Newspaper Archive.

These locally produced Rolls or Books of Remembrance can be found through many avenues: local libraries, the Imperial War Museum or National Army Museum, the originating organisations themselves (particularly schools, universities or businesses) or through the usual online genealogical sites. Some are available through open-source digital libraries, like www.archive.org, and it is well worth doing an Internet search on the home town, employers or educational establishments linked to your ancestor. There is also a website dedicated to listing Rolls of Honour and memorials at www.roll-of-honour.com.

DOMINION AND COLONIAL TROOPS
If your ancestor served in one of the non-British contingents in Egypt or Palestine, their records will probably be with their parent country. However, there is one exception to this rule.

Indians
A substantial number of Indian Army troops served in Egypt and Palestine. The majority of the troops who kept Egypt safe from the autumn of 1914 through to the end of 1915 were Indian, while many more were posted to Palestine in the spring and summer of 1918. At that point, large numbers of British troops were withdrawn from Palestine and sent to France, where they were desperately needed to staunch the German breakthrough on the Western Front, and all bar one of the divisions in the EEF became mixed Anglo-Indian units. The usual method was to have three Indian and one British infantry battalions in each brigade, while the British cavalry were re-brigaded with one British and two Indian cavalry regiments.

The Indian Army was a separate entity to the British Army, reporting to the Viceroy of India, and within it there were several sub-divisions. Most units were part of the centrally controlled Indian Army, but others were detachments from some of the semi-independent principalities of India. These were known as Imperial Service Troops, and although they were supervised by the Indian Army, their training and equipment was not always to the same standard. One example would be the Bikaner Camel Corps, which arrived in Egypt in 1914 under the personal command of Maharaja Ganga Singh, the ruler of Bikaner. This remarkable man had already led his troops, under broader British command, in the Boxer Rebellion in China in 1900 and in Somaliland in 1902–4.

Many of the officers of the Indian Army – and all above a certain rank – were British, and their records survive at the British Library in series IOL L/MIL/14. Unfortunately, the records for Indian officers and for other ranks were kept in India, and are not known to survive. The War Diaries are held at TNA, and mention some individuals.

Australians

The most famous Australian units to serve in Egypt and Palestine were the ALH. Actually Mounted Riflemen – organised as cavalry but trained to ride into battle and then fight on foot, they were not equipped with swords until 1918, although they did carry out a famous mounted charge before this at Beersheba, on 31 October 1917. With their distinctive slouch hats, in some regiments improved with a plume of emu feathers, easy discipline and aggressive attitude, the ALH have become a significant pillar in Australia's First World War 'Anzac legend'.

However, the ALH were far from the only Australians to serve in the theatre. In late 1914 the barely trained Australian Imperial Forces were sent to Egypt for intensive instruction and to be turned into effective combat units. The infantry went to Mena Camp and the ALH to Meadi (or Maadi) Camp, both just outside Cairo. From there, many were sent to Gallipoli in April 1915, but their base remained in Egypt and all of their replacements were sent to the Cairo camps for training, just as wounded men were brought back to recover. Only in early 1916 did the bulk of the Australian forces, including the training camps and several ALH regiments, get sent to France.

Australian personnel are extremely well documented, by British standards. Records of Service are held at the National Archives of Australia (www.naa.gov.au). These contain everything the British ones should, and are accessible online. There is also extensive genealogical advice on the same site.

A wide variety of records are also available through the Australian War Memorial (www.awm.gov.au). These records include copies of

Men of the 10th Australian Light Horse taking part in the capture of Jerusalem, December 1917.

embarkation rolls, muster rolls, honours and awards, prisoner of war files, as well as a wide selection of collections of personal papers. These are all accessible through an excellent search engine. The Australian Official History of the First World War and unit War Diaries are also accessible through the site.

Advice and further information can be gathered through the Australian Light Horse Studies Centre (http://alh-research.tripod. com). Although this site does not seem to be getting actively added to any more, it still contains a wealth of information. There is also an ALH Association (www.lighthorse.org.au), with lots of resources and information, and an active forum.

New Zealanders
Less well known, the New Zealand Mounted Rifles Brigade (NZMRB) fought alongside the Australians throughout the war, and took the lead in much hard fighting. Like the Australians, they had

been sent to Egypt very early on to be trained, establishing themselves at Zeitoun Camp just north of Cairo. Again, this served as a base for the Gallipoli operations, and then remained as a British training camp from 1916 onwards. The NZMRB were also trained to ride to battle and then fight on foot, although again like the Australians they saw much mounted service as scouts or cavalry.

A lot of NZMRB records are available through Archives New Zealand (http://archives.govt.nz), including Records of Service, muster rolls, details on honours and awards, courts martial records, casualty records and some War Diaries, although it has to be said that their search engine is not the easiest to use.

The Auckland War Memorial Museum's Cenotaph Database is a complete, searchable database of the New Zealanders who served in the First World War. It is a work in progress, and those who were killed are better covered than those who survived. A significant amount of biographical (pre- and post-service included) and medical information is included. This can be found at www.aucklandmuseum. com.

There are also two good websites for further information on the New Zealand contribution to the First World War at www.nzhistory. net or more specifically on the NZMRB at www.nzmr.org.

South Africans
The South African 1st Infantry Brigade served in Egypt for several months over the winter of 1915–16, seeing some extremely hard campaigning against the Senussi tribesmen in the Western Desert.

Records of Service for men who served with the South Africans can be obtained from: South African National Defence Force, Documentation Service, Private Bag X289, Pretoria 0001, South Africa; sandfdoc@mweb.co.za. You may also find some interesting information from the South African Military History Society (http://samilitaryhistory.org/index.html).

TRENCH LIFE

Although the campaigns in Egypt and Palestine can be characterised by broad, open spaces, trench warfare still went on. Generally, it was a pale comparison with that on the Western Front; lines were generally less complex and the barbed wire less prolific, although one exception was the areas south of Gaza in the summer and autumn of 1917. Here the Ottomans dug in deep and well, using the ground excellently and employing not only barbed wire but also thick cactus hedges in front of their lines. In fact, the Ottomans generally excelled at making defensive lines. When Brigadier General Sir Guy Dawnay visited the sites of the actions at El Magdhaba and El Magruntein, on the Egypt–Palestine border, he was amazed. At El Magruntein he found 'a splendidly selected position on a small rise in a gently rolling, grassy plain; absolute "glacis" slopes all round – not a mouse could move up to attack it without being seen from ever so far.' At El Magdhaba, the Ottoman 'works around the place were the most cunningly sited I have ever seen. You can't see them at all till you absolutely walk into them. Our artillery could never pick them up.' (Letter to his wife, 10 March 1917, IWM 10403). Usually the Ottomans were very short of barbed wire, especially in late 1917 and throughout 1918, and this weakened their positions.

The British dug extensive trenches and redoubts along the Suez Canal from the outbreak of the war until well into 1916. Life here could be idyllic. Apart from the usual 'stand to' at dawn, attitudes were fairly relaxed, and soldiers could bathe or fish in the Canal, or even just sit and watch the ships go by, like New Zealander S. Nautch of the 1st Battalion, Canterbury Regiment:

It is a wonderful thing to sit and watch the approach, the passing and the fading away of these monsters of the night. The canal [is] a perfect mirror reflecting the stars overhead and the cliffs of the opposite bank. Away to the north the canal stretched straight for 7 miles, away to where sea and sky appear to meet, and the stars of the heavens appear to mingle with their reflections in the waters. (S. Nautch, IWM 12330)

Further into the desert, things were more fraught. As the EEF advanced across the Sinai temporary defences were dug. Usually these were strings of posts rather than continuous lines, and had little or no barbed wire, making them very vulnerable to attack. Occupying them could be nerve-wracking:

Bir el Abd was now the most forward infantry post. It was half-way between Kantara and el Arish – so that the 'spear head' of the offensive defensive was making good progress. It was defended by a great ring of outpost positions, each held by a platoon or so, usually with another platoon in support. Night after night we slept in clothes and boots, with our equipment on us, and woke at intervals to peer into the dark for an hour, or see that others peered – then two more hours' sleep and another turn of duty – and so on till we were called for stand-to – variously at three, four, five, or six am, as the season changed. Then we all stood ready, rifles loaded and bayonets fixed, denied cigarettes or conversation, lest our positions be given away to an approaching enemy . . . till at last the desolate world revealed itself, empty as ever and, to the jaundiced eye of a fasting man, utterly abominable. (*5th Battalion Highland Light Infantry*, p. 114)

South of Gaza proper lines were established over the summer of 1917, although once a few miles east of the city they changed into a string of redoubts and outposts, placed to watch over the wadis and valleys that might be used by an Ottoman force to sneak into the British lines. British and Ottoman infantry patrolled no-man's-land at night, while the cavalry of both sides patrolled further out on the eastern flank night and day. Trench raids were

Men of the Norfolk Yeomanry digging a trench near the Suez Canal, a major operation.

mounted to gather intelligence or stir up the Ottomans, although quieter patrols also went out to listen to and locate the enemy. Sergeant Thomas Minshall of the 10th Battalion, King's Shropshire Light Infantry, took part in one such patrol:

Another evening volunteers were asked for to reconnoitre a portion of 'no man's land', important information being required about a particular part of the enemies position, two officers, two sergts, and twenty five men were required. Of course, 'yours truly' must be in the little 'stunt' . . . I was sergt in charge of the supporting party, Sergt P., Major T., and three other men were to push on when we arrived at a certain point, and do their utmost to obtain the necessary information. Turkish patrols were very likely to be encountered so we went fully prepared, not only for that reason, but to support our comrades should they be attacked or surprised. My little party consisted of ten riflemen, bombers and bayonet men, Lewis gunners, and stretcher bearers. We set off under cover of darkness marching by compass and stars. Only a few hundred yards beyond our barbed wire, shots informed us snipers were about, so changing our direction to avoid them, we arrived at the first place we wished to find, unchallenged. Here my men were to wait in readiness while the small party advanced so I arranged them to the best of my ability in case of emergency. Everything worked out fine, the Major and his party were successful, they returned to us in fine spirits, and we all 'about turned' and reached our trenches before Mr Moon gave our little game away. I omitted to tell you, we all carried two bombs each, besides rifles etc., so should we have been surprised, required, or encountered a patrol, we wouldn't have been a very pleasant party to meet, and although game for anything our object was not to raid, but to obtain as much information as possible without being seen. (Thomas Minshall, IWM 2792)

Once in the Judean Mountains and the Jordan Valley, trenches were harder to dig, and instead rocks would be piled to create 'sangers', or positions protected by a stone breastwork. Often, these sangers were placed on the peaks of steep hills, with the only support being on the peaks either side. Although these could fire across valleys to support each other, it could take hours for reinforcements to climb up the mountains to help.

The inside of a trench on the Suez Canal defences, very different to those in France.

Chapter 5

CASUALTIES

The forces in Egypt, Palestine and Syria suffered around 600,000 casualties, and of them only around 50,000 were due to wounds inflicted in battle. And those are just the serious casualties – deaths, or wounds or sickness bad enough for a soldier to be removed from his unit for more than a few days. It is very unlikely that your ancestor did not at some point have to report sick for an upset stomach, a toothache or far worse.

COMMON COMPLAINTS
We will look at the different levels of medical care shortly, but first it is worth considering the primary problems with healthcare in the EEF. Hygiene was, of course, a major issue. While biological matter (everything from bodily waste to dead animals) would usually quickly desiccate in the hot sun, limiting the spread of disease, the vast swarms of flies that drove everyone mad ensured that at least some harmful bacteria was spread around. Stomach complaints were fairly common – between 2 and 3 per cent of the EEF suffered from dysentery throughout the war, and while about 3 per cent of the troops went down with diarrhoea while they were in Egypt, this went up to 7.5 per cent when the EEF was in Palestine. As much as anything, these complaints would be caused, or at least exacerbated, by the men ingesting small but constant amounts of sand in their food and water.

Water was, of course, always in short supply. As we've seen in Chapter 3, each man only received a pint of water per day for hygiene, and that was only under the best of conditions. Sometimes this could be supplemented by brackish ground water from a few feet under the sand, or by bathing in the sea, but this was infrequent. Keeping a man's body clean was a problem, but so too was keeping his uniform clean. Army uniforms were not known for their silky smoothness at the best of times, but after months of having sweat and sand ground into them they could become as stiff as a board and as rough as sandpaper. Around cuffs and at other points where equipment rubbed, they could wear deep sores into the skin and flesh underneath. Likewise, metal that had become hot under the sun could inflict small burns when it came into contact with skin. Troops were told to paint their metalwork black or green partly to stop this happening, although it also had the added benefit of stopping the sun glinting off the metal and giving away troops' positions to the enemy.

These sores could only be fully treated by frequent washing with plenty of fresh water, the shortage of which was the main problem in the first place, and so most were just bandaged and left to heal in their own time. As a rule, only if they became infected would a man be withdrawn from the line for proper medical treatment.

Skin complaints could also come from another source: venereal disease, or VD. This was widespread in Egypt in 1914 and 1915, as tens of thousands of young men poured into the country, fired up with the excitement and novelty of their situation, and away from home and the constraints of their families and communities. Their amorous intentions were given ample opportunity to exercise themselves among the bars and brothels of Cairo and Alexandria, where prostitution was a growth industry. Alcohol was also a growth industry, with much of it (even those bottles wearing well-known labels) being brewed in highly insanitary local stills. These strong and impure drinks added their own health problems, but could also lower inhibitions alarmingly, causing men to go astray who would never usually do so. Statistics do not exist for 1914 or 1915, but by 1916, when the problem was being brought much more under control, about 7.5 per cent of the army in Egypt reported with VD. This tailed off drastically in 1917 as the army moved into the desert, far from temptation, to just 2.8 per cent, although after the capture of Jerusalem and several other large towns at the end of 1917, the rate rose again to 5 per cent in 1918.

Malaria was another serious issue, particularly in late 1917 and throughout 1918 and 1919. Before the irrigation and land reclamation schemes of the last seventy years, much of the coastal region and the areas around the major rivers of Palestine turned to marsh after the winter rain. In the Jordan Valley the problem was even worse with large numbers of pools of standing water littering the landscape. In these areas, mosquitoes bred in huge numbers, and malaria rates were extremely high, reaching around 13 per cent of the army in 1918. This was the average throughout the year. In the spring and the summer it was much higher, but a concerted campaign was waged by the army to eradicate the problem. Pools and marshes were drained, rivers and streams cleared and 'canalised', and small labs set up all around the army where blood samples could be taken and the disease diagnosed within hours, allowing rapid and effective treatment.

CASUALTY PROCESS

Malaria was not the only disease or injury to receive swift treatment. Each battalion or cavalry regiment had its own First Aid Post, a doctor known as a Medical Officer, some orderlies to assist him and a detachment of stretcher-bearers. In battle, the stretcher-bearers would go out and bring in the wounded for treatment, although it could take hours for them to bring everyone in. While in the rear or on duty holding the front line, anyone who was sick would report to the Aid Post, usually for the morning sick parade. If the problem was small, it would be dealt with at the Aid Post by the doctor. If it was beyond the facilities or resources of the Aid Post, the man would be sent back to brigade level.

Each brigade had a Field Ambulance. These were larger and better equipped than the Aid Post, with more staff, a small number of permanent beds in a tent and the ability to perform minor surgery. They also had additional stretcher-bearers who could be sent forward to support the regimental teams, and could be separated out into Main and Advanced Dressing Stations, so as to provide more support closer to the units in their brigade. If the Aid Post was for applying first aid, in action the Field Ambulance would focus on stabilising the patient. Surgery could and would be performed to stop bleeding and make sure that patients had the best possible chance of making the trip back to the next stage without dying.

Behind the Field Ambulances were the Casualty Clearing Stations (CCS). In France, there would be one of these per division, but in Palestine the system was slightly different due to the lower numbers of troops involved. Lower numbers meant that the troops were less densely packed into the landscape, with divisions being spread out over wider areas. In the first half of 1917, there were just two CCSs supporting the army on the Gaza–Beersheba line, a frontage of around 25 miles. This could leave a wounded man with a lengthy trip from his brigade Field Ambulance back to the CCS, and so from July 1917 the numbers were steadily increased to a total of seven CCSs and a single Indian Clearing Hospital – the Indian Army equivalent of a CCS. By September 1918, by which time many of the British troops had been replaced by Indian Army units, the EEF boasted five CCSs, two Indian Clearing Hospitals and four Casualty Clearing Hospitals, the latter of which catered for both British and Indian troops.

Each CCS was essentially stationary, with tented wards for around 1,000 patients, and various specialist staff such as dentists. Here, major surgery would be carried out, including such operations as amputations. Indeed, before the 3rd Battle of Gaza in the autumn of 1917, extra surgeons and other surgical staff were sent out from the hospitals in Egypt to bolster the CCSs. Patients would stay here until they were fit to make the long journey back to proper hospitals in Egypt. Again unlike France, the distances were such that the movement of men even by train back to hospitals was a lengthy process.

Finally, possibly many days after being wounded or falling seriously ill, a soldier would find himself in a hospital ward in Egypt.

The Base Hospitals in Egypt were divided into General Hospitals and Stationary Hospitals, although the differences were essentially meaningless. Some were based in or on existing Egyptian hospitals, including some of the specialist mobile hospitals that in peacetime toured Egypt dealing with specific problems, or in the military hospitals that supported the usual garrison. Others were set up in available buildings, with hotels being a popular choice for obvious reasons, and some of the biggest and most prestigious hotels in Egypt were taken over for the duration. Again, the numbers of these were expanded in 1917, from three Stationary Hospitals and seven General Hospitals in early 1917 to eight and eleven respectively by the end of the year. By September 1918, the system had expanded to include ten Stationary Hospitals in Palestine and four in Egypt, twenty-five General Hospitals in Egypt, ten hospitals specifically for prisoners of war and a host of other specialist units for dealing with specific diseases or parts of the body.

All of these hospitals could prove a haven after months in the desert, or in the case of Private William Lindsay of the Royal Scots at Gallipoli. However, as Lindsay recorded in a letter home in August 1915, military hospitals still followed some elements of military routine:

> The hospital is in three blocks and is situated in large grounds. It was up till recently a private school and when I say grounds I mean playgrounds. We are not allowed to go outside and all we see of Eastern life is viewed from the top of a wall where we sit in the cool of the evening. Two pyramids can be seen from the ward in which I'm in.
>
> 6 a.m. Reveille. Get up, wash and make bed.
>
> 7.30 Breakfast. Those on full diet go to dining hall, remainder dine in ward.
>
> Till 9.30 Help sisters and orderlies in tidying ward.
>
> 9.30–11 Doctor's rounds
>
> 12.30 Dinner
>
> 4.30 p.m. Tea

9 p.m. Bed

I'm dressed in a shirt, pyjamas, socks and slippers and find it quite warm enough. We lie on our beds most of the day. Reading is our one and only way of passing the time. The Cairo newspapers are absolutely worthless and contain no news of Britain but we get some English papers a fortnight old . . . I'm making fine friends here and though life is sometimes monotonous we are having a quiet and happy time. Last Sunday evening I went to church service. It was a Church of England minister and the service was very enjoyable. (William Lindsay, IWM 11765)

As well as the above units and hospitals, the army also had a host of Sanitary Sections to work on everything from the proper positioning of latrines to the clearing of dead bodies after battle, a wide range of laboratories and eleven hospital trains.

MOVING THE SICK AND WOUNDED

Sick and wounded men would move up and down this chain of units. Minor ailments could see them only move back a short way and return to their unit within days. Major wounds could see them take days to get back to Egypt, and then spend weeks or months in hospital. Unless a wound was permanently debilitating, it was very unlikely for a man to be sent back to the UK (or Australia or New Zealand). Instead, once fighting fit they would be sent back to the front.

Movement between the different sections could be on a variety of means of transport. Horse-drawn wheeled ambulances were used, but sand carts became more common as the war progressed. These were essentially ambulance sleds, with skis that skimmed over the sand and (theoretically at least) provided a much smoother ride. They had canvas covers over the top to provide shelter for the men sitting or lying inside. They could also be quite a rough ride, but were nothing compared with cacelots. These were wooden boxes – disturbingly like coffins – that were strapped one either side of a

Inside a ward of Nassich Hospital in Cairo, 1916.

camel's hump. A man could sit or lay in a box, again protected from the sun by a canvas awning. Unfortunately, the swaying gait of a camel made the boxes pitch and roll as it walked, inducing feelings of seasickness in those being carried. They were unpopular to say the least. Motor ambulances were also used, although the numbers available were fairly small and the rough roads in Egypt and Palestine took a punishing toll on the engines and tyres.

For longer distances, men could be placed on a train. By 1918 the army had eleven designated hospital trains, fitted for carrying wounded men on racks in each carriage and with a small medical staff. However, in 1916 men were just as likely simply be placed in empty freight cars, sometimes open-topped. Captain Oskar Teichman, the Medical Officer of the Worcester Yeomanry, broke his leg at the Battle of Romani in August 1916, and was disgusted by the facilities:

> This 'hospital train' consisted of one engine and a number of open trucks, the latter containing nothing – not even straw . . . The stretcher cases were placed on the floor of these trucks, while the walking cases sat on the sides. When we started off there was the usual 'bump, bump, bump' which one hears from a goods train, and pitiful groans escaped from the badly wounded and fracture cases. (Teichman, *The diary of a Yeomanry M.O.*, pp. 78–9)

CASUALTY EVACUATION IN ACTION

During battles, the system easily became swamped. Trooper Patrick Hamilton served with the Field Ambulance of the 4th Australian Light Horse Brigade. He recalled the aftermath of the attack on Beersheba on 31 October 1917 in terms that would not be out of place on the popular US TV series *M*A*S*H*:

> In the operating tent our medical officers worked steadily and almost in silence. Continuous skilled surgery hour after hour. Anaesthetics, pain killing injections, swabs, sutures, tubes in gaping wounds, antiseptic dressings, expert bandaging. The medical orderlies did a fine job assisting.
>
> Stretcher bearers were standing by for the change-over. Two on either side lift the stretcher clear of the stands, and replace it with the next patient all within two minutes. The pace never slackened!
>
> Here, out in the field at night, surgical work of the first order was performed. This was the 4th Light Horse Field Ambulance at work! About 2 a.m., after six hours of dedicated work by all hands, the last of our 45 wounded was put through. All patients by now were bedded down under canvas and made as comfortable as possible. Most slept through sheer exhaustion or under drugs. We arranged shifts and lay down

on the hard ground fully clothed for a few hours' rest. (P.M. Hamilton OBE, *Riders of destiny: The 4th Australian Light Horse Field Ambulance 1917–8* (Gardenvale, Mostly Unsung Military History, 1995), pp. 67–8)

During the big advances of late 1917 and late 1918, the casualty movement system could easily break down. The supposedly mobile units would become inundated with men, who then had to be treated and kept until transport came to evacuate them further back. Delays led to medical units being split, with some of the staff advancing with the army while others stayed behind to care for the existing patients.

Beersheba War Cemetery.

RECORDS FOR CASUALTIES

Records for wounded personnel are very limited, at least as far as working out how they moved through the system described above. Although it should be easy enough to work out the Aid Post and Field Ambulance from the soldier's unit, during periods of heavy fighting this system was liable to become confused or disorganised. Unit War Diaries are unlikely to record the names of individual soldier's receiving aid, even less so if it they were only treated at the unit Aid Post and never technically left the unit. Totals may be given for the killed, wounded or evacuated sick each day during battle or each month during quieter times, but it is unlikely for anyone but officers to be named.

In the Records of Service that survive, there is a Form B103 'Casualty Form – Active Service', but this is misleading. It in fact records all of the soldier's movements between units, although in the case of his being evacuated wounded or ill, it may contain an entry for which CCS he was sent to. More likely, it will just record the Base Hospital that he ended up in. There is a limited number of hospital registers at TNA, also now available on Forces War Records, and those that relate to Egypt seem only to refer to those men who were invalided all the way back to the UK and were discharged from the army. The registers of the Silver War Badge are also worth looking at, for men who were invalided all the way home.

Otherwise, details on how a man was killed or wounded are hard to find. The unit War Diary will show roughly what was going on that day, and may even pin down a casualty to a particular action or event. Some regiments or battalions kept ledgers recording the basic details of each man's service, and these sometimes survive at regimental museums. The museum of the Queen's Own Worcestershire Hussars (Yeomanry), for example, have ledgers that give, among other things, detailed information on illnesses or wounds. The registers of the Silver War Badge, discussed in an earlier section, can also provide limited information.

HOW THEY FOUGHT: THE INFANTRY

The way that infantry fought in the First World War is forever captured in the popular imagination by the images of long, dense lines of heavily laden infantry walking slowly into enemy barbed wire to be mercilessly mown down by machine-gun fire. Like many images of the First World War, this one is often misunderstood.

In France, enemy positions were sometimes only a matter of yards away, and certainly this could also be the case in the mountains of Palestine, where the rocky hillsides made combat a deadly game of hide and seek. More often, on the plains and deserts, enemy positions would be several miles away, and a long, steady advance was needed even to reach a point where the attackers could shoot back. With miles to cover, even under heavy artillery and machine-gun fire, the troops had to walk in order to preserve their energy. Their heavy packs would be left behind, and they would usually only carry what was immediately needed, although this had to include the heavy burdens of extra ammunition, rations and possibly water, as it could take many hours or even days for resupply columns to catch up to them. From the middle of 1917 steel helmets also began to be issued, adding a further torment as the sun beat down on them.

As they covered the distance to the objective, each infantry platoon would form a column four men wide, the quickest and easiest formation for covering ground fast. Once artillery and perhaps long-range rifle and machine-gun fire began to reach them (say, at 2 miles) the single column would disperse into four, widely spaced columns or perhaps loose 'blobs' to make a smaller target. Once within a mile or so of the enemy and in effective range, they would swing into lines, each man three paces from the men either side. Before the summer of 1917, these lines would advance until within close range of the enemy before going to ground. Alternate sections would dash forward while the

British infantry dishing up a meal in camp.

remaining sections gave covering fire, and then vice versa. In the summer of 1917 the EEF was retrained in methods learned on the Somme the previous year. Each platoon was reorganised and the four sections became: Machine Gun Section, Sniper/Scout Section, Bombing Section and Rifle Grenade Section. Under the new scheme, the Sniper/Scouts and the Bombers (armed with large numbers of hand grenades) would go in front, with the Machine Gun and Rifle Grenade (modified hand grenades launched from the ends of rifles, giving them a longer range) behind. If they ran into an enemy position, the Machine Gun and Rifle Grenade sections would lay down covering fire while the other two sections worked forward, lobbing hand grenades and keeping up an accurate rifle fire. If they could not advance, they would move around the enemy's flank under the covering fire. Likewise, platoons next to each other would move around the flank of any enemy positions holding up the sections on either side of them.

The battlefield was a confusing place. As the troops moved rapidly around the landscape, the only reliable means of communications were by voice or written messages conveyed by a 'runner'. To call up artillery or other support could takes hours as the runner had to find the right people to pass the request to, and then perhaps hours more for the reinforcements to travel the distance needed.

Sergeant W.M. Town MM of the 1/5th Essex Regiment recalled the attack on Gaza in early November 1917:

> At that moment the signals came to 'Advance!'. Then it seemed that an absolute inferno was let loose . . . so loud was the uproar that we were unable to hear the bursting of Johnny's shells, or the whistle of their bullets as they opened fire on us.
>
> At last through the haze of smoke, we saw the Turkish line, and prepared to make a final rush. At that moment however, men were seen standing on the Turkish Redoubt which our Company had been ordered to take. A disaster was avoided just in time by the order coming along that they were our own men, and that we were to enter the trench further along, otherwise we should have opened fire on the men, and probably caused heavy casualties.
>
> The order was given to charge, and we set up a yell with such wind as we had left, and charged through the wreckage of 'Johnny's' wire. . . . Well, we piled into the trenches, and set to work to clear away any Johnnies left . . . I found myself in a communications trench, which led into a deep hollow, and there were quite a few Turks dodging about that hollow. Needless to say, I also 'let drive' with my rifle, and it was quite exciting for a time.
>
> [The next dawn] 'Abdul' got excited, and his machine guns started ripping the sand bags on the trench to pieces. We had to lie flat because the trench was very shallow, having been almost obliterated by our artillery . . . Shortly afterwards we had to withdraw from our part in the communications trench, it having become untenable. We got out by wriggling and squirming along, dragging the

British troops in a trench on the Wadi Ghuzze, south of Gaza.

Lewis gun and magazines with us. We managed to find a fairly comfortable part of the trench, and settled down again. Thirst was an awful drawback. For the first forty-eight hours we had only what water we had brought in our bottles, and the men were in a state of semi-stupor by the time we got the glad news that several petrol tins of water were being sent up at night. (W.M. Town MM, IWM 15018)

Meanwhile, Private William Hendry of the 2/14th London Regiment ('London Scottish') had been fighting among the Ottoman positions on the road to Beersheba:

By this time our water was right out and rations very short. I must have looked like a baboon, not having shaved or washed for over a week. Now we were to attack one of their most formidable positions, a very high and long ridge. Away we went from our cover, quite in day light. They instantly spotted us, about a mile away. We got into artillery formation (commonly known as blobs) and quickly advanced through a din of splitting shrapnel. It was a splendid sight to look back and see all the blobs moving steadily forward, with shrapnel bursting over-head, and as if nothing was happening, and the German gunners which the Turks had, desperately trying to stop our advance by firing hundreds of shells into the air. It was really astonishing the number of shells that burst right above us, and caused so few casualties . . . Now we were within bullet range, so opened out, three yards separating each man, they were spitting up all around us now, when suddenly the fellow on my left went down with a bullet in the centre. I stuck his rifle in the ground so that the stretcher bearers would not miss him. We were getting near the front of the hill now, when I noticed blood on my tunic and found my chin bleeding. I dropped into a crack in the ground, broke my iodine bottle and well spread it over my chin, putting a bandage on. While I was doing this the bullets were raining down on the ground around, but only my legs were exposed. I jumped up quickly and ran on to catch up [with] the company, when I suddenly felt a sharp pain in my arm and blood was trickling into my hand, but I did not stop this time and caught my platoon at the foot of the hill. Up we went firing at any slight object ahead. Our machine gunners got going also and covered our advance firing from the flank. When we arrived at the top we found the Turks had fled from their trenches, which we occupied firing hard at the retreating Turks . . . Now we looked around to see our company sadly thinned, and luckily my arm looked worse than it really was. I could not tell the exact extent of my chin wound, as my head was well coated with sand and congealed blood, but neither of them hurt. (W.N. Hendry, IWM 6873)

Chapter 6

RESEARCHING UNITS

Before we examine how to find out more about different units, it might be best to look at how they were organised, and some of the basic terminology involved.

THE EGYPTIAN EXPEDITIONARY FORCE

The highest functional level in the British Army was the Expeditionary Force, such as the British Expeditionary Force (BEF) in France, the Mediterranean Expeditionary Force (MEF) that had fought at Gallipoli and of course the Egyptian Expeditionary Force (EEF) itself. The BEF consisted of several Armies, but both the MEF and EEF were small enough to effectively be an Army in and of themselves. Armies consisted of several Corps (each under a Lieutenant General), and there would eventually be three of these within the EEF: XX and XXI Corps, both infantry, and the Desert Mounted Corps (DMC). These were formed in the summer of 1917. Before that everything was a bit of a mess, with the Desert Column commanding a mixed and changeable force of infantry and cavalry divisions doing the actual campaigning in the Sinai Desert. The rest of the divisions were in the rear protecting the Suez Canal or the lines of communication and supply, coming under various other higher formations.

From the summer of 1917, each Corps consisted of several divisions, although they also had a contingent of 'Headquarters troops'. These consisted of various specialist troops – signallers, logistics staff and transport columns, and engineers – and they also had a large body of artillery that could be deployed to support attacks along any part of the Corps' line. The HQ troops also included small forces of infantry and cavalry, which could be used either for guard duties in the rear, for scouting for the Corps commander or as an immediately available reserve which could be thrown into an attack or a defence without the delays that sending orders down through the chain of command in the levels below the Corps would inevitably suffer.

Below the Corps was the division, which consisted of about 20,000 men for the infantry, and was commanded by a Major General. Each division contained three brigades, and also had their own substantial artillery force, as well as other support and specialist troops in the same vein as the Corps – signallers, engineers, logistics and transport staff, veterinary staff and a machine-gun company.

Brigades, commanded by Brigadier Generals, are where things start to get complicated. There were basically three different types, for infantry, cavalry and artillery.

Infantry Brigade

For the infantry, each brigade consisted of four battalions, plus a trench or 'heavy' mortar battery which provided very short-range artillery support. Generally, through the British Army, brigades very seldom consisted of four battalions of the same regiment (all explained below!). However, in the EEF there were several examples of this; the 161st Brigade of the 54th (East Anglian) Division consisted of battalions only from the Essex Regiment, while the three brigades of the 60th (London) Division all came from the London Regiment. (Without wanting to make things too complicated, the London Regiment is an oddity as well, in that it did not have a higher, regimental formation. In fact, it had no regular battalions either, being the only purely TF (i.e. part-time soldiers like today's Army Reserve (formerly the Territorial Army)) regiment in the British Army. Instead, the different battalions were affiliated with different areas of London and other regular units.)

The two divisions named there also show another feature of the divisions of the EEF: they were strongly territorial. In fact, they were territorial in that all were formed of units from the TF, and no complete regular army battalions served in the EEF. Six of the eight infantry divisions that served with the EEF up until the spring of 1918 were made up of battalions almost entirely from specific regions: 10th (Irish) Division, 42nd (East Lancashire) Division, 52nd (Lowland) Division, 53rd (Welsh) Division, 54th (East Anglian) and the 60th (London) Division. Of the other two divisions, the 74th (Yeomanry) Division was formed of yeomanry cavalry units that had fought on foot at Gallipoli and had then been converted to infantry afterwards, and the 75th Division was formed of various units from all around the UK.

In the spring of 1918, everything changed as the Germans broke through on the Western Front, and many of the British units in the EEF were withdrawn to France and replaced with Indian troops. The 52nd and 74th Divisions were sent to France in their entirety, but all of the other divisions (except the 54th Division) simply lost three out of every four battalions, which were replaced by Indian troops. Thus, each brigade then consisted of one British and three Indian battalions. Two new Indian divisions, the 3rd (Lahore) and 7th (Meerut) Divisions, also arrived, but these too were one-quarter British.

Now for the battalion (under a Colonel or Lieutenant Colonel). For the British and Anzacs, this consisted of just over 1,000 officers and men, divided into four companies (under a Major or Captain) of just over 200 men, plus a battalion headquarters. Each company was divided into four platoons (under a Lieutenant), each of which was divided into four sections (under a Sergeant or Corporal). Each battalion had small sections of specialist troops attached; medical staff, signallers (and, later, wireless operators) and from late 1915 members of the Machine Gun Corps with heavy machine guns (before then, the machine-gunners had been members of the battalion).

The basic infantry weapon was the .303in calibre Short Magazine Lee–Enfield (SMLE) bolt-action rifle. This was rugged and accurate, had a ten-round magazine and came with a bayonet. Machine guns were also issued. The 'heavy' types, initially the Maxim but later the

Vickers Machine Gun with a four-man crew, were used by battalion level units which could be moved around to where they were needed. Each platoon later had its own 'light' machine guns with two-man crews, either Lewis Guns or the French Hotchkiss Gun. Both of these lighter types had magazines with open sections that could easily become clogged and jammed in sandy conditions.

Battalions were usually numbered as part of a larger regiment, although this latter was a largely administrative designation. As a rule, the 1st and 2nd Battalions of a regiment were the regular troops, the 3rd and 4th Battalions the part-time soldiers of the TF, and the 5th and 6th Battalions the nominal formations of the Reserves (soldiers who had served as regulars, and were bound to act as a reserve force for a set number of years). With the massive expansion of the army in 1914, many new battalions were established. The TF was meant only for home defence and not obliged to serve overseas, but the vast majority volunteered to anyway. As a result, a 'second line' of battalions was established to take their place. The original units, with a '1/' prefix, were despatched to the war, while battalions with a '2/' prefix were raised at home. Many of these units, once fully trained, were despatched overseas and a 'third line' ('3/') were raised in their place. Many of these third-line units would be sent to the front later in the war, and a fourth line established at home. The Indian, Australian and New Zealand forces had a straightforward numerical system of units, and the above system should not be confused with the Gurkha system of having multi-battalion regiments. For example, the 2/7th Gurkha Rifles refers to the 2nd Battalion of the 7th regiment.

Cavalry Brigade

The cavalry brigade, meanwhile, was much smaller, with just three regiments, plus an artillery brigade and some signallers, engineers and logistics staff. The yeomanry (British TF cavalry) were grouped into brigades on a regional basis. Initially, their titles reflected this, but in 1916 they were renamed in a more pragmatic way. For

A nice clear view of two of the cap badges identify these men as being from the Suffolk Yeomanry.

example, the 1st South Midland Mounted Brigade became the 5th Mounted Brigade.

Unlike the infantry, for the cavalry a regiment was a battlefield unit. As a note on terminology, technically the British, Australian and New Zealand cavalry were not actually cavalry. They were Mounted Rifles, who were organised as cavalry but were intended to ride into battle and then fight on foot, although they would act like traditional cavalry when it came to scouting before and after battle, and even occasionally fight mounted.

In peacetime, cavalry units did not have separate equivalents to battalions, although some formed second line units after the outbreak of the war. A regiment consisted of just over 500 officers and men, divided into 3 squadrons of 150 men plus a headquarters and a machine-gun section. Each squadron was sub-divided into four troops, and each troop into sections of four men. These men would ride four abreast on the march. In action, one of those four men would lead the horses of the other three to safety while they fought. Obviously, this greatly weakened the fighting strength of the unit.

Like the infantry, the cavalry were armed with the .303 SMLE rifles, although the British cavalry (and the Australian and New Zealanders from 1918) also carried the 1908 pattern Cavalry Sword. The cavalry also had machine guns. A Machine Gun Squadron with Maxim or Vickers Machine Guns (carried in carts) was attached to each brigade, while each squadron had a single Lewis Gun until the spring of 1917, when these were withdrawn and instead each troop received a Hotchkiss Gun, greatly improving each unit's firepower.

The Imperial Camel Corps were Mounted Infantry, in that they were mounted, but equipped and organised on the same company and battalion pattern as the infantry. There were four battalions, any three of which served together as the Imperial Camel Corps Brigade, while the forth was on detached garrison and patrol duties in Egypt. These battalions rotated that duty.

Artillery Brigade

Finally there is the artillery brigade, which is a group of three batteries. The artillery was split into several groups. The Royal Horse Artillery (RHA) was fast moving, using horses to quickly move lighter guns that would give close support to attacks. The Royal Field Artillery (RFA) was also horse-drawn but had heavier guns for harder pounding, generally more sedentary and further back from the front lines. The Royal Garrison Artillery (RGA) operated the big guns, drawn by tractors and mostly used in static positions, such as coastal defences or fortresses, although they also had some of the larger battlefield guns and mortars. The Indian forces also had Mountain Artillery, which were light guns (sometimes known as 'screw guns') that could be dismantled and carried to otherwise inaccessible areas on the backs of elephants, camels or mules. Artillery forces were usually organised into batteries of six field guns (or four for the RHA) or four howitzers, which could be further split into Sections of two guns.

ORDERS OF BATTLE

The exact way that all of the above units were organised as a hierarchy is called an Order of Battle, or ORBAT for short. It is important to know where exactly within the great mass of an army your relative actually stood. You are unlikely now to find out which squad or platoon they were in (although clues such as they were a machine-gunner may have been passed down) and even knowing which company or squadron they were in can be a matter of luck. However, if you can trace their battalion/regiment/battery/unit, you can start to put them into their correct place. From there, you can find documents on that particular unit and work upwards through the brigade, division and corps to find out exactly where they were and what they were doing, which actions they may have fought in and what their particular contribution to victory was.

ORBATs are the best way to trace this lineage. They appear in the 'Official History of Military Operations in Egypt and Palestine', compiled by the army in the 1920s, and a snapshot from the autumn

A view of the 6th Battalion, Manchester Regiment, in Alexandria, December 1914.

of 1918 appears in General Allenby's despatches, which were later published as 'The Advance of the Egyptian Expeditionary Force'. These sources are also, of course, very useful for tracing the movements of units and obtaining narratives of the different actions, but if you are just interested in the ORBATs for now, it is as well (and cheaper) to simply search online. Websites like The Long Long Trail have ORBATs for each division, while a comprehensive set of ORBATs for the EEF can be found on Wikipedia.

WAR DIARIES

Armed with information on their unit and place in the hierarchy, you can start tracing your ancestor's unit. There are several sources available for this, and it is a matter of personal preference which you start with. War Diaries are often cited as the best sources available for units, and this is true to an extent, although you do run the risk of getting bogged down in detail quite quickly. Regimental histories, where available, can give a good overview and better equip you to then navigate the War Diaries.

The War Diary is the monthly diary of each unit at infantry battalion/cavalry regiment level and higher. A well-kept War Diary will give a day-by-day narrative account of the unit's movements, actions and the arrival and departure of its members. It should also include copies of routine orders, and possibly the orders and plans relating to specific battles or raids. Unfortunately, they have been 'weeded' at some point and a lot of the routine material that should be enclosed has been removed, while the general level of detail in the narrative can vary greatly. Partly this depends on the enthusiasm or dedication of the junior officer tasked with keeping the War Diary, who may have been less than enamoured with the extra work and administration it created. It also obviously depends on what else was going on. At a time of heavy action or prolonged fighting, the War Diary may become quite scant as the keepers would have had other priorities, although equally you find many that have clearly been filled in, in some detail, after the action.

While diaries are supposed to be kept daily, they were often completed at the end of each month, and details such as the movements of personnel are added in at the end of the month, regrettably usually just as total figures, although officers sometimes get named. Therefore, it is always worth checking the whole of the month, and not just the day you think your relative arrived, was wounded or died. Equally, sometimes the important information is left until the end of a stint in the front lines rather than the end of the calendar month. Whereas troops in France went through a well-established routine of (roughly speaking) four days in the front line, four days in the reserve trenches and then four days resting behind the lines, in Egypt and Palestine the lower tempo of operations tended to mean units held the front lines for much longer periods. For example, the 1/4th Battalion, Royal Sussex Regiment held their section of the front south of Gaza from 31 July to 25 August 1917. Only on being relieved by the 1/4th Battalion, Essex Regiment does the War Diary record:

The enemy showed little artillery activity on the Battalion front during this period. A few small shells were fired at the front line trenches, but only 2 casualties were suffered, two men wounded, one of whom afterwards died of wounds.

Patrols were sent out nightly from our own lines towards the enemy wire, and pamphlets printed in Turkish were left in conspicuous places.

The enemy appeared to send out very few patrols. One enemy Patrol was fired on by our sentries, and the Warrant Officer i/c of the Patrol came in and gave himself up as a deserter.

One other deserter gave himself up during this period.

> 200925 Pte. H. Booker   ) were accidentally killed by the
> 200929 Pte. L. J. Hards   ) explosion of a Turkish shell head
> (TNA WO 95/4631)

In fact, Booker had been killed on 9 August and Hards had died of wounds the next day, but the incident was not mentioned on those days, only in the summary two weeks later.

This kind of omission regarding individual casualties is unfortunately not uncommon. The 2/10th Battalion, Middlesex Regiment launched a trench raid in a neighbouring section of the line on 15 August 1917. The War Diary entry states:

> 2 Officers and 2 Platoons rush Sugar Loaf with the bayonet, killing all Turks who showed fight and pursuing the remainder with fire as they fled to Beach Post. At the same time a party of 30 enemy attempted to work round our right flank and rush L[ewis] G[un] covering that flank. These were dispersed by L.G. fire from Bacons Boil and Stokes Gun from support line. (TNA WO 95/4632)

What they do not mention is that Private Albert Frederick Robert Smith, aged 20, from Edmonton, London, was killed in the attack.

(Incidentally, Bacons Boil was a small hill, and a Stokes Gun was a type of trench mortar.)

It is also worth working upwards, to brigade level. They would give precis of the actions of their constituent units, and it is also possible they will have copies of the plans for or reports on raids and attacks. These often include casualty returns submitted as part of those reports, which can give far more detail than the battalion does, such as a full list of names.

Another way that War Diaries can be useful is giving map co-ordinates for where things are happening. This can be particularly helpful for Egypt and Palestine. Some areas are quite featureless and a map co-ordinate is the only way to pinpoint a location, but more of a problem is that local names tend to get horrendously garbled. Partly this is due to British inability to cope with foreign names, especially those written in a foreign alphabet, but it is not helped by the fact that they were working on maps largely compiled by asking local residents what things were called. The names were usually written phonetically and in several different ways at the time, and have sometimes changed drastically over the intervening hundred years, especially as names get later translated into Hebrew in Israel. In many cases, the British simply assigned their own names – like the Bacons Boil seen above – to landmarks.

Therefore it is invaluable that the War Diary of the 1/4th Royal Sussex Regiment quoted above also says that their part of the line was in square Q9a88 on the Gaza–Tel el Sharia map. Most of the army's standard 1:40,000 scale maps have been preserved in series WO 303 at TNA. Each of these maps should have a three-digit reference, but usually the actual places that it covers are used as a title, as in this example. Each 1:40,000 map was divided into 6,000yd^2 blocks, each lettered from left to right, top to bottom. That is the 'Q'. Within each 6,000yd^2 box were 36 1,000yd^2 boxes, this time numbered but again from left to right and top to bottom. In this case, that is the '9'. Within each of the 1,000yd boxes were 4 500yd^2 boxes, again left to right and top to bottom. These were lettered and in this case it is the 'a'. And, finally, along the bottom and side of each of these smallest boxes were the numbers 1–10, working up or right from the bottom left-hand corner. On these, where the lines from 2 '8's intersect, is where the unit was based.

Incidentally, this grid system had been invented in the BEF in France quite early in the war in order to improve accuracy in direction of artillery and the movement of troops. The idea was not put into practice in Egypt and Palestine until the spring of 1917, but it is, of course, now almost inconceivable for any map not to be divided into some form of grid.

The primary set of War Diaries is held at TNA, although they have been conducting a long-term project with Naval & Military Press to digitise the whole collection. At the time of writing the Western Front and Gallipoli have been completed, and work on the other fronts is in progress. Once complete, they will be available for downloading (usually as monthly blocks for each unit) for a fee from TNA, or printed versions of each units diary will be produced by Naval & Military Press. It seems probable that a CD-ROM of all of the units for Egypt and Palestine will be marketed as well (as it was for the Western Front), but this is likely to be expensive.

REGIMENTAL (AND OTHER) HISTORIES

The other source for the history of a particular unit is the regimental history. These can take several forms, some of them of more use than others. Many regiments, and indeed individual battalions, commissioned histories after the First World War, although in a few cases the war was simply folded into a much longer work on the entire history of the unit. Needless to say, the details in those types of works can be a little scant. However, for the most part the focus is the war, although the approach can still vary. Some regiments, such as the Norfolk Regiment, cover all of their battalions in a single volume, with only a few chapters on the units in Egypt and Palestine. Others, such as the Royal Welsh Fusiliers, were much more ambitious and produced a series of volumes covering the war in some depth, with a whole volume dedicated to the 'other fronts'.

However, arguably the best histories are those that focus on a single unit. For cavalry regiments this is not a problem, and units such as the Queen's Own Worcestershire Hussars (Yeomanry) and the Sherwood Rangers Yeomanry, or any of the regiments of the New Zealand Mounted Rifles, have excellent histories. For the infantry, though, it depends very much on the enthusiasm of the battalion's officers (mainly) as to whether a battalion history was compiled. The end results can vary in both approach and readability. Many are quite formal, sticking to the facts, but others can also adopt a more chatty style and be packed with anecdotes. The history of the 1/5th Battalion, Highland Light Infantry, for example, can be highly recommended to anyone who wants to know more about what the infantry experienced in Egypt and Palestine, as it not only covers the facts but it is also a highly entertaining read. A quite different, but still very interesting, book is the history of the 1/5th Battalion, Essex Regiment (*With the 1/5th Essex in the East*) which was written by the commanding officer and largely takes his perspective, so it also includes a fascinating insight into the problems and challenges of leading and commanding a battalion on a First World War battlefield.

Histories of other types of units are altogether rarer. The 1/1st Hants Battery, Royal Horse Artillery, produced their own (very thin) history, and the 74th Field Ambulance produced one in the 'packed full of anecdotes' style, with contributions from many different members.

There is, to the best of the author's knowledge, only one infantry brigade history from the EEF, which covers the 161st ('Essex') Brigade, although the ALH produced histories of some of their brigades, while the official history of the New Zealand Mounted Rifles (*The New Zealanders in Sinai and Palestine*) is a brigade history by default, as they only had the single brigade. However, most of the infantry divisions have good histories: 42nd (East Lancashire), 52nd (Lowland), 53rd (Welsh), 54th (East Anglian), 60th (London) and 74th (Yeomanry) Divisions all commissioned histories after the war that are worth reading. The 10th (Irish) Divisional history unfortunately only covers Gallipoli. None of the cavalry divisions have histories, but the mounted troops do have the only Corps history, in R.M.P. Preston's excellent *The Desert Mounted Corps.*

Regimental (and other) histories used to be rare, expensive and highly collectable. However, over recent years publishers such as Naval & Military Press have reprinted them by the score, while many are also available in digital format through online libraries or sites such as www.militaryarchive.co.uk.

Naval & Military Press have also put a lot of effort into reprinting memoirs of officers and men who served in Egypt and Palestine, as has the publisher Leonaur (www.leonaur.com). While naturally the literary merit of some of these varies greatly, they are an excellent way to find out more about the experiences your relative may have gone through. If you are lucky, you will find a memoir from their unit, but even a memoir by a soldier in a different unit but of the same type (i.e. infantry, cavalry, artillery, etc.) will shed significant light on their lives.

REGIMENTAL MUSEUMS
A final place to look for information on units is the regimental museum. There are hundreds of these across the UK, with all levels of access, displays and records. Some, like the Royal Buckinghamshire Hussars (Yeomanry), occupy only tiny corners of the local town museum, in this case the Buckingham Old Gaol Museum, although their display does include the very impressive painting of their charge at El Mughar on 13 November 1917, by Thomas Dugdale. Others enjoy their own building or collection, or at least a large, dedicated section of one. The Royal Welsh Fusiliers, for example, have an excellent museum in two towers of Caernarfon Castle, although unfortunately the shape of the towers leaves less room than could be desired, and the section on the First World War tends, naturally, to give most attention to the battalions on the Western Front and, of course, their famous war poets.

Increasingly, regimental museums are merging. This is a natural result of the amalgamations that have been a regular part of the

British Army's existence since the 1960s. Some recently merged regiments combine the museums of their parent units. Others take a geographical approach, with the units in a particular area pulling together regardless of a complete lack of any military ties, as has happened in Gloucestershire and Worcestershire. Naturally, this dilutes the collection and leads to even more competition for limited space, but these moves also often allow for modernisation and to put the collections on a much more secure footing for the future. When the Worcestershire Regiment and the Queen's Own Worcestershire Hussars (with Worcester City Council) came together to form the Museum of the Worcestershire Soldier, the yeomanry were able to greatly modernise and expand their First World War display, which includes not only many artefacts from the war in Egypt and Palestine, but also a life-size model of a Yeoman in normal desert marching kit on his horse, making it one of the best EEF-related displays in the country. The Keep Museum in Dorchester has some displays on the Senussi campaign and the Imperial Camel Corps, and also has a life-size model of a Dorset Yeoman, in this case an officer charging.

The amount and quality of material on display in museums obviously varies greatly, although of course each artefact does help shed a little bit more light on your relative's experiences, while models such as the Worcester Yeoman can really bring to life how they looked and what it must have been like. Likewise, the amount of archival material available also differs. Most units will at least have copies of their own histories, and additional sources such as regimental journals and relevant books. Most will also have photograph albums, perhaps memoirs or collections of papers, and other material relating to a specific campaign or period. Many will have copies of some official documents as well, although of course the primary set of War Diaries is at TNA. It may be worth your while writing to the relevant museum, most of whom now charge for research.

The Army Museums Ogilby Trust (www.armymuseums.org.uk) maintains a list of all of the existing regimental museums, with brief details on their collections, links to their websites and basic information on their locations and opening hours.

There are also the national military museums. At the time of writing, the National Army Museum is closed for refurbishment, and it remains to be seen how much relevant material they will put on display. Their collections include a huge number of diaries and collections of letters, although their Reading Room never used to be the easiest to access or to use. Perhaps this will change.

The Imperial War Museum has recently redeveloped its First World War galleries, removing the labyrinth of small rooms that were packed with artefacts, including a lot of very interesting EEF material, and replaced them with a darkened, open-plan floor with lots of interactive maps and video displays. The focus is almost entirely on the Western and Home Fronts, with all of the others fronts being lumped together into one, not very large corner. However, they do have an excellent research collection including not only diaries, letters, etc., but also a superb selection of regimental histories, and the Oral History collection which contains interviews with EEF veterans. Their Reading Room has been under threat of closure recently and is now suffering from several restrictions, but it is still worth the effort if you want to do some serious research. Large parts of their excellent photographic collection are available online.

The RAF Museum at Hendon also features letters, diaries and photo albums from men who served in the RFC, RNAS or RAF in Egypt and Palestine. (See Chapter 9 for more details.) Again, services have recently been restricted, but their Reading Room is still one of the friendliest and easiest to use. They also of course have examples of many of the aeroplanes used in that theatre.

HOW THEY FOUGHT: THE CAVALRY

The British cavalry are much maligned in First World War history, and greatly misunderstood. In a war of machine guns, barbed wire and (later) tanks, it is easy to see them as an old-fashioned waste of resources. In fact, the speed with which cavalry could move, as well as the shock of their sudden arrival, came in useful even in France, with successful cavalry actions on the Somme and elsewhere. In Egypt and Palestine, they were absolutely invaluable.

The cavalry had three main roles: scouts and patrols, mounted riflemen and shock troops. The first role was vital in Egypt and Palestine. In defensive terms, the front lines were usually thinly held, and the desert flanks wide open. Cavalry were needed to patrol these areas constantly in order to stop enemy forces sneaking up on the EEF. In offensive terms, the cavalry were also needed to go out in front and find the enemy, then fixing them in place (by attacking) until the infantry and artillery could come up to destroy them. Both of these tasks could only be done by cavalry, who could cover large distances in relatively short periods, and had the speed to rush back to their own lines with reports quickly if need be. It was gruelling work, often meaning days and nights on end away from the comforts of camp, with the constant worry about getting lost in the featureless desert, or running out of water (horses needed some 30 litres/6.5 gallons per day). It was also skilful work, as the enemy would try to ambush patrols, just as the British, Australian or New Zealanders would try to ambush enemy patrols.

As mounted riflemen, the cavalry would be expected to mostly fight on foot. In real terms, a cavalry brigade usually only had the firepower of roughly a single infantry battalion, but they could be thrown into an attack or to bolster a defence to act as normal infantry if need be. More often, they would be used to surprise or harass an enemy. A force of horsemen could appear out of the dawn to surround an Ottoman unit who had thought themselves

The magnificent statue to the ALH in Beersheba.

miles from danger, as happened frequently in the Sinai in late 1916, or during the last great advance in late 1918. Given the relative lack of firepower of the cavalry, this element of surprise was crucial. However, this mobility could also be used to fight superior numbers of enemy troops by harassing them. During the 1st Battle of Gaza, March 1917, a single squadron of the Queen's Own Worcestershire Hussars did just this to hold off a much larger column of Ottoman reinforcements heading for Gaza:

> 'A' Squadron came in contact with them soon after 1pm, and, for the next four hours, this squadron was engaged upon some very pretty cavalry fighting. The heads of the

columns were not met frontally, but they halted mechanically as a brisk fire from a troop broke out on their flank. Slowly the Turks deployed to the threatened flank, only to find the cavalry vanished into space while fire opened upon them from another troop, this time in their rear. This method of defence adopted by 'A' Squadron, admirably handled by Major Ffrench-Blake, was fluid to the last degree, but it was most effective. Harried this way and that by their mobile opponents and never given the opportunity to indulge in a frontal fire fight, where their numbers would have given them the advantage, the enemy were unable to make any progress, until finally they gave it up and marched sulkily back to Sharia. ('C', *The Yeomanry Cavalry of Worcestershire, 1914–1922* (Stourbridge, Mark & Moody Ltd, 1926), p. 89)

The most spectacular use of the cavalry was as shock troops, charging home into the enemy with swords drawn. Seemingly suicidal in the days of modern artillery and machine guns, this could in fact still be a devastatingly effective way to break an enemy rear guard or take a well-dug-in position. Several such charges took place in Egypt and Palestine, including at Agagia (26 February 1916, Queen's Own Dorset Yeomanry against the Senussi), Beersheba (31 October 1917, ALH (using bayonets instead of swords) against Ottoman trenches), Huj (8 November 1917, Queen's Own Worcestershire Hussars and Warwickshire Yeomanry against Ottoman rear guard), and El Mughar (13 November 1917, Queen's Own Dorset Yeomanry and Buckinghamshire Yeomanry, against well-dug-in Ottoman trenches). All of the enemy forces involved were well equipped with machine guns, and all but the Senussi also had field artillery (particularly at Huj). These charges could be costly, but not as much as may be expected.

Perhaps the most familiar image of a cavalry charge these days is the dramatic and (cinematographically) magnificent charge in

Steven Spielberg's film version of *War Horse*. However, this is wrong in almost every detail. The lines of charging horses would be well-spread out (not with the riders knee-to-knee, as depicted in the movie), while there would also be a large gap between the front line and those behind, to allow following riders to swerve around casualties in front. It was also common for the horses to suffer higher casualties than the riders. Soldiers (especially machine-gunners) are trained to fire at the centre of the mass of the target, and in the case of a mounted man that is the horse's chest, while the rider is a much smaller target. Spielberg's lines of empty horses galloping through the woods is very poignant, but also highly misleading.

The speed with which the cavalry moved meant that in almost all cases the defenders could not adjust their sights quickly enough and as they got closer, more and more enemy bullets and shells would go straight over their heads. The charges were also devastatingly effective, with the morale effect of having sword-wielding riders on horseback smashing into their positions being enough to make any troops panic.

2nd Lieutenant J.H. Blaksley, recalled the charge at Agagia:

We were spread out in two ranks, eight yards roughly between each man of the front rank and four yards in the second. This was how we galloped for well over half a mile straight into their fire . . . At first they fired very fast and you saw the bullets knocking up the sand in front of you . . . But as we kept getting nearer, they began to lose their nerve and (I expect) forgot to lower their sights. Anyhow the bullets began going over us and we saw them firing wildly and beginning to run; but some of them – I expect the Turkish officers – kept the machine guns playing on us . . .

The Senussi were running in all directions, shrieking and yelling and throwing away their arms and belongings; the Yeomen after them, sticking them through the backs and slashing right and left with their swords . . . Some stood their ground, and by dodging the swords and shooting at two or three yards' range first our horses then our men, accounted for most of our casualties. (Marques Anglesey, *A history of the British Cavalry 1816–1919*, Vol. 5, *Egypt, Palestine and Syria 1914 to 1919* (London, Leo Cooper, 1994), p. 31)

Sergeant J. Hayden of the Warwickshire Yeomanry described the charge at Huj:

We came into range of their guns which sounded like a roar of thunder, they seemed to have turned every gun they had onto us at one moment. Men and horses were pitch-polling on either side of me, I expected my time was coming every second. The dust was so thick we could not see the horse in front of us . . . By this time our squadron only numbered 25 unhurt . . . I was shot, it caught me in the face, within 30 yards of the guns, I thought to myself I am only hit slightly as I could still see out of both eyes, but after a few minutes my left eye stopped up with blood. We were 10 or 12 [left] by now and carried on without a check . . . I galloped round the guns like Lord Nelson with one eye blocked up . . . As we surrounded their guns there were Turks under each gun with all hands up, quite clear from the reach of my sword and all surrendered. I was then making for a bit of cover, and had only cantered about 30 yards from the guns when a machine-gun opened fire on me from the left rear, shooting my horse through the head and neck, as he dropped he fell across my leg and foot, pinning me down. (Pritchard Collection, Museum of the QOWH)

Chapter 7

PRISONERS OF WAR

Some 16,583 British and Indian troops were taken prisoner by the Ottomans during the First World War. Most – about 13,000 – were captured in one go when General Townsend's force at Kut El Amara in Mesopotamia was forced to surrender after a long and painful siege, with many of the garrison succumbing to starvation. Smaller numbers were captured at Gallipoli, and in Egypt and Palestine. A total of 3,290 of them are known to have died in captivity, although nearly 4,500 others who were known to have been captured by the Ottomans were simply never heard of again.

Their experiences as prisoners would vary greatly, partly based on their rank (which denoted to some extent their treatment), but also on the whims of their gaolers and the physical geography of their surroundings. The majority of prisoners were taken into the mountainous regions of Anatolia, in modern day Turkey. With the dilapidated state of the Ottoman transport system, simply getting there proved a challenge. Thousands of the men captured at Kut El Amara, already weakened by the siege, died along the way.

Once in Anatolia, officers and other ranks were separated. The luckier other ranks prisoners would be assigned as orderlies to the officer's camps. The less lucky ones were often put into their own cramped, uncomfortable camps in the mountains. Food was supplied on the same scale as for Ottoman other ranks, and was of poor quality. Clothing, extra food and other necessities from soap to candles had to be bought by the prisoners themselves, for which they received an allowance in Turkish Pounds (£T). The British government forwarded them £T10 a month from their pay, and the

British and Australian troops captured during the 2nd Battle of Gaza, April 1917.

Ottomans offered a further £T1 per week to those willing to work for them. This meant relief from the boredom of camp life, and a chance to earn extra money that could buy the food and other necessities that could make the difference between life and death. Many jumped at the chance, although many others were simply conscripted.

The working parties faced hard labour in grim conditions. The most common tasks were building roads and railways through the mountains, where the main supply routes from Constantinople ran down to Syria, Palestine, Mesopotamia and Arabia. The poor state of these routes caused constant delays and problems in moving troops or keeping their front lines supplied, and the Ottoman government was constantly trying to improve them. Unfortunately for the prisoners, it involved working in alpine conditions while still wearing their desert uniforms and using barely adequate tools.

Sickness and death rates were high. Medical care was rudimentary, and a man refusing to work was more likely to face a beating or even a flogging than be referred to a doctor.

Then as now, the International Red Cross (IRC) monitored conditions, but being separated into small parties in largely inaccessible areas made this very difficult. At best the IRC could make sure that post and parcels of comforts arrived regularly, but as the Ottoman guards were fed and clothed as poorly as the prisoners themselves these were likely to be stolen. Equally, escape from the working parties was almost unthinkable. In their weakened condition, and with no chance to build up the supplies needed to support an escape, the mountains were more effective gaolers than their Ottoman guards.

Officers faced betters odds of escape. The obstacles involved were considerable. Lieutenant Elias Jones recalled:

> The real sentries were the 350 miles of mountain, rock and desert that lay between us and freedom in every direction. Such a journey under the most favourable conditions is something of an ordeal. I would not like to have to walk it by daylight, in peace-time, buying food at villages as I went. Consider that for the runaway the ground would have to be covered at night, that food for the whole distance would have to be carried, and that the country was infested with brigands who stripped travellers even within gunshot of our camp; add to this that we knew nothing of the language or customs of the people and had no maps. (Elias Jones, *The Road to En-Dor* (London, Bodley Head Ltd, 1919), pp. 54–5)

Officers usually had slightly more means with which to build up supplies for an escape attempt, and occasionally small groups of officers would make a bid for freedom, exploiting the fact that most of the guards (known as 'gamekeepers') were old men or those who had been rejected from front-line service on health grounds, and whose already low motivation was compounded by boredom every bit as great as that of their captives. The usual escape route was to the north, to reach the Russian forces in the Caucasus.

Most escapees were rapidly caught, and brutal retribution would be poured onto the offending camp. Lieutenant Jones teamed up with RFC officer Cedric Hill, and exploited an act that they had worked up to help relieve the boredom in the camp, and ended up making an escape that puts almost any of the other First World War (or indeed any of the more famous Second World War) attempts in the shade. They had made an Ouija board, and had become adept at faking seances. Their highly superstitious camp commandant had heard of their exploits, and in return for better billets and treatment they had agreed to act as intermediaries between him and the spirit world. Eventually, they convinced him that they were in contact with the spirit of an Armenian who knew where a vast treasure had been buried. In April 1918 they convinced the commandant to search for the treasure, and the two officers led a small party off into the mountains. After months of wandering, they arrived in Constantinople in August, and Jones and Hill managed to get themselves committed to hospital. After a further six weeks of incredible hardship, they were declared to be lunatics, and were liable for compassionate repatriation. It almost seems a shame, after all that they had been through, that the war ended before they could sail for home. Both left memoirs – *The Spook and the Commandant* (London, William Kimber & Co. Ltd, 1975) by Hill and *The Road to En-Dor* by Jones – which are well worth a read.

The majority of personnel simply resigned themselves to captivity and waited. The lot of the officers was easier in many ways, but still far from comfortable. The 'camps' were usually just a clutch of commandeered houses in an isolated village. Typically, the first intake of officers would be constrained to one house, often crammed in with barely room to sit or lie down, until perimeters could be established and the newly appointed commandant came to terms with his duties. At Yozgad, for example, all of the officers and their orderlies were initially confined to two large houses, with simple holes in the floor of one room to act as latrines (leading to an outbreak of typhus). It was days before the guards would let the prisoners take it in turns to stand on the doorstep, and longer still to take even a few steps outside the door. Eventually, after several months a small compound was established including several houses, the lane between them and then into the fields on either side. The slightest transgression would still see the prisoners re-confined for days on end, and the process of expansion begin again. Meanwhile, each officer had to pay rent for his accommodation.

Unlike the other ranks, officers also had to pay for their food, and so they received a larger allowance: the equivalent of 4s a day from the Ottoman government, and £T18 per month from the British. As well as rent, this had to pay for the purchase and preparation of their food. In many camps a supplier was appointed by the commandant, but this system was wide open to corruption, and inflated prices led to many camps insisting on being able to buy their own food directly from the local markets. Even here, prices soon rose. Most of the hamlets used were isolated and farmed their land at subsistence levels. The arrival of hundreds of new mouths to feed stretched them to the limit. In August 1916 the equivalent of a standard daily British ration (¼lb beef, 1¼lb bread and 8oz potatoes) cost an officer 2s 6d. By January 1918 the same officer was paying 36s for the same ration, and some items, such as tea, had risen in price by over 1000 per cent. As well as food (and tea), he would also have to purchase clothing, candles, firewood, milk, sugar and anything required to vary this bland diet.

Under the Geneva Convention officers were not allowed to work to supplement their wages, and the Red Cross began to add their own, ever increasing allowance to the pay of the officers. Food parcels could be sent from home, from both individuals and committees. The families of men at the different camps soon set up their own associations, with printed newsletters being circulated with extracts from letters, advice on where to buy the best items for food parcels, and appeals to club together to buy books or even gramophones and records. Government bodies also provided relief for prisoners, and some organisations such as the Victoria and Albert Museum offered book supply services.

Parcels from home were often looted by the guards, but enough got through and even if the contents were stolen the wooden boxes could be used to build furniture or feed fires. Frequently officers had to rely on money sent from home, or through cashing personal cheques either with local shopkeepers or various amenable embassies. The American, Swiss and Netherlands embassies in particular provided material as well as financial assistance.

Simply passing the time was one of the major problems. The boredom and inactivity, the confinement and privations that they were suffering were never far from their minds, and depression often lurked nearby. Lieutenant George Wright wrote home:

> Will it ever end? To walk about here during a beautiful sunny day I often think what an awful waste of time it all is, and what a beautiful day it would be if I were only at home free to go where I liked instead of meeting a sentry at the end of the path with a rifle 'This far shallt thou go and no further'. Oh for peace again, when there will be no more destruction and killing and waste. To be free again, to write a letter without having to think whether I can say this or that without fear of having my letter torn up, to do useful work again and not waste day after day with nothing attempted & nothing done, to eat decent food and drink decent liquid once more; I shall have learnt to appreciate every good thing by the time I get back to it again.(Wright letters, QOWH Museum)

Some men could escape purely in their heads, dreaming of the lavish meals that freedom would bring, or the places they would be able to go. Others needed more active ways to occupy their minds. Some activities could be found to kill two birds with one stone, passing the time and supplying food by growing crops or keeping poultry.

Expert help was often at hand. Prisoners included men from all branches of the army, as well as the navy and air services, from all kinds of backgrounds and all across the Empire. Lecture series and classes were set up to share knowledge and keep brains active. Lieutenant Arthur Holyoake found that the essentially civilian character of the war-time army was a boon in this area: 'Those [talks] given by regular army officers were all on technical army subjects, but the Yeomanry and the War time people provided some very interesting & entertaining evenings. Herbert on 'Tea planting', Ward on 'Trapping in Canada', Jones on 'Crime in Burmah' [sic], Highett on 'Bees' etc.' (Holyoake memoirs, QOWH Museum).

Libraries were established in many camps. Initially, prisoners simply shared and then pooled their books, but soon specific requests and orders were being sent home for manuals and technical books on anything from farming to electrical engineering. Literature also led to theatres being set up from scrounged materials, while concerts could also be improvised. Some performances were lower brow than others, and scripts often written in the camps themselves, full of pointed barbs at their guards or conditions to vent their frustrations. Such occasions could be improved by the liberal provision of homebrewed alcohol.

Sports were another natural pursuit, where space could be found, with footballs and other equipment coming in through the neutral embassies or from home, or being built in the camps. At Yozgad, the Ottoman guards made hockey-sticks to sell to the prisoners, raising money to supplement their own wretched rations. In some camps, prisoners could offer their parole (their words as officers and gentlemen not to try to escape) and could, under escort, walk or even ski (on improvised equipment made from floorboards) in the mountains.

By far the highlight of camp life was the arrival of mail. Being cut off from news of home drove many nearly to distraction, and all appreciated the arrival of anything that provided something new and different to look at and think about. Although letters were censored, fevered imaginations would try to pull all that they could from them. Lieutenant Jones:

Mail Day at Yozgad meant visits. The proper thing to do, after giving everybody time to read their letters several times over, was to go from room to room and pick up such scraps of war news as had escaped the eye of the censor. Some of us received cryptograms, or what we thought were cryptograms, from which we could reconstruct the positions on the various fronts (if we had imagination enough), and guess the progress of the war. The news that somebody's father's trousers had come down was, I remember, the occasion of a very merry evening for it meant that Dad's Bags (or Baghdad) had fallen at last. (Jones, *The Road to En-Dor*, p. 9)

With the surrender of the Ottoman Empire at the end of October 1918, most of the prisoners were simply released from the camps, and left to make their ways to Constantinople. Here, RN ships waited to pick them up and bring them home.

RECORDS

There are two commonly available lists of prisoners of war, the first issued by Cox & Co. covering officers only, and the other being that produced by 'The British Red Cross & Order of St John of Jerusalem', covering all ranks. These are found in most of the big libraries and archives, and the July 1917 edition of the latter has been reprinted by Naval & Military Press. In the Cox & Co. list the details provided are basic, giving the name, rank, date of capture, date of repatriation or death where applicable and the country where they were held. The Red Cross list is much more detailed and covers both officers and other ranks, giving their basic service details and dates, but also not only their battalion but also often their company and sometimes even which platoon they were in – information that is almost impossible to find elsewhere.

There are also various files in the Foreign Office papers at TNA that deal with prisoners of war or with their treatment or the conditions within the camps, including FO 383/231, FO 383/336 and FO 383/456. Some of those files are also available through Find My Past.

There is an excellent guide to prisoner of war records through the Families in British India Society (FIBIS) website: http://wiki.fibis.org/index.php/Prisoners_of_the_Turks_(First_World_War). There is also a Facebook page, 'Descendants of PoW in Ottoman hands WW1 (Esir Torunlari)', where the descendants of prisoners exchange information.

HOW THEY FOUGHT: THE ARTILLERY

The artillery were the undisputed kings of the First World War battlefield, even more than the dreaded machine gun. They came in different types and sizes and with a variety of ammunition, all used for different purposes on the battlefield, and until the summer of 1917 they were always in short supply in Egypt.

The lightest were the trench (or 'Stokes', after the manufacturer) mortars, batteries of which were attached to every brigade. These were small enough to be used inside trenches, lobbing mortar bombs in steep curves so that they could fall almost vertically down into enemy trenches, or on positions hidden in wadis or behind rocks.

The RHA were light units, using 13-pounder 'Q.F.' guns. Q.F. stood for 'Quick Firing', because they used shells like giant bullets, being thrust into the breach of the gun in a single piece. (On the bigger guns, usually the shells and the propellant were loaded in separately and rammed up into the barrel.) They could indeed fire very fast, and as they were usually used with the cavalry could move fast too. They had a crew of nine men and were pulled (with a limber to carry the ammunition) by teams of horses, dashing into combat and unlimbering for use at short ranges. Because shells fell in an arcing trajectory, aiming guns was something of a science (aided by complicated sights), and light guns could fire up to 5,900yd/5.4km. At close ranges, the trajectory was flat and sights unnecessary, so this was known as firing 'over open sights'. RHA batteries were often TF units, and kept strong county or city identities.

The RFA had the bigger guns, usually 18-pounder 'Q.F.' field guns and 4.5in 'Q.F.' howitzers. These were heavier and slower to move, but still horse-drawn. The 18-pounders were bigger versions of the 13-pounders, with ranges up to 11,000yd/10km in later models. The heavier shell packed a bigger punch, and these would be used to support the infantry in attack and defence. Like the 13-pounder, they had a range of ammunition including high-explosive shells (which exploded on impact) and shrapnel (which burst before impact, sending out fragments of metal). It could fire up to twenty (but usually many fewer) 18.5lb (8.4kg) rounds per minute. The 4.5in howitzer lobbed shells in an arc, like a giant mortar. It had a shorter range than a field gun (7,300yd/6.7km) but could fire over sand dunes, hills or mountains to drop shells down on the enemy behind. It could fire four 35lb (16kg) shells per minute.

The RGA used the biggest guns, including the 60-pounder and the 8in howitzer, for battering enemy positions. These were much heavier and harder to move, needing tractors to tow them. The 60lb gun fired two 60lb (27kg) rounds per minute, while the shell of the 8in howitzer weighed 200lb (91kg), and with both the shell and the bag of propellant being rammed in separately. RGA batteries were often much smaller than RHA or RFA ones.

Being an artilleryman was hard work. The guns, limbers, horses and tack needed constant care and attention. Physical effort was often needed to help the gun over or past obstacles. In the soft sand of the desert, 'pedrails' (small planks of wood) were added to the wheels to increase the surface area and stop them sinking in, but even so, Anthony Bluett recalled, 'an eight-horse team could with difficulty pull a gun and its limber over fairly level ground; frequently twelve horses were required and sometimes as many as sixteen!' (Bluett, *A Gunner's Crusade*, p. 31).

In the Judean Mountains and other places, the horse teams from whole batteries sometimes had to be combined to pull a single gun up a hillside, due to the poor condition of the horses as well as the steepness of the rocky slopes. The EEF had a single

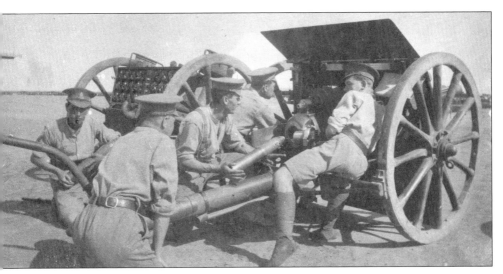

A RA field gun in action.

unit of 'mountain guns', the Hong Kong and Singapore Battery (actually Indian troops), which were small and were carried in pieces on the backs of mules or camels. They were short range, and the unit was known as the 'Bing Boys' due to the strange sound they made when fired.

Frequently, the pace of the advance of the EEF was dictated by the time needed to bring up the guns, with troops working frantically to improve or build from scratch roads and paths for them to move along. The infantry would only be able to advance so far before getting beyond the range of their own guns, and would halt until they were brought forward. Forward Observation Officers were attached to infantry and cavalry units, and used various signals (flags, mirrors, sometimes telephones, but the wires were fragile and difficult to manage) to call up and then direct artillery support. Aircraft or tethered balloons could also direct fire.

Before big attacks, the artillery would systematically pound enemy defences, roads, stores and artillery positions (just as enemy 'counter-battery fire' would try and knock out the British guns). They worked to carefully prepared and timed plans, throwing a certain number of shells at a certain target for a certain time before moving on. Rates of fire were usually much slower

A gun of the Hong Kong and Singapore Battery.

than the maximum possible, to save wear on the barrels which, if they became too hot, could become distorted. And, of course, this also saved wear on the gunners themselves.

During one of the Trans-Jordan raids, in May 1918, the Hants Battery RHA recorded:

> On the morning of the 4th a bombardment of enemy positions, of one hour's duration, was maintained. Fire was commenced on Makkar Derbasi, at the rate of one round per gun per minute for ten minutes, and subsequently increased to the rate of two rounds per gun per minute.
>
> The bombardment drew fire from the enemy; one other rank in No. 1 gun was slightly wounded and two horses in the wagon lines were hit. During the morning, and up till 1 pm, various targets were engaged. (*1/1st Hants Royal Horse Artillery* (Uckfield, Naval & Military Press, 2005), p. 57)

Likewise, before the Battle of Megiddo in September 1918:

> The barrage table having been prepared during the previous days, full preparations were made for the 19th, which was the date selected for an advance.
>
> One hundred and fifty rounds had been allowed for registration and 220 rounds per gun were dumped at each gun-pit. These were carefully sorted into heaps and lots, each heap having the exact number of rounds required for each lift of the barrage. (*1/1st Hants Royal Horse Artillery,* p. 63)

Chapter 8

IN THE AIR AND ON THE SEA

The air war over Egypt and Palestine was very different to the more familiar one over the Western Front. The numbers involved were much smaller for a start, with the British peaking at just seven squadrons (one of them Australian) in 1918. The tempo of the war was also lower. A small British unit had been sent to Egypt in November 1914, and an Anglo-French seaplane unit set up at the same time to operate off the coast. Both used old and obsolete aircraft, but then the first German aircraft did not arrive in Palestine until April 1916. This unit, Flieger Abteilung (FA) 300, was half the size of either of the British squadrons in the theatre at the time – No. 14 Squadron RFC and No. 1 Squadron Australian Flying Corps (AFC) (also known as No. 67 Squadron RFC). However, the Germans had far better aircraft until the end of 1917. Although the numbers on both sides meant that combat was relatively unusual, when aircraft did clash the British and Australians seldom stood much chance. It was even worse for the RNAS, whose East Indies and Egypt Seaplane Squadron had taken over coastal patrol work in the spring of 1916, and whose seaplanes were made ungainly by their large floats.

Only in the summer of 1917 did the RFC attached to the EEF begin to expand, having four squadrons by the end of 1917 and beginning to receive better aircraft. However, the Germans also received reinforcements over the winter of 1917–18, and it was only in the summer and autumn of 1918 (by which time the RFC had become the RAF) that the British won air superiority. By the end of the war, the RAF in Palestine consisted of Nos 14, 111, 113, 142, 144

An RFC DH1a in Egypt.

and 145 Squadrons, as well as No. 1 Squadron AFC. No. 17 Squadron
briefly served in Egypt in 1915–16.

Flying was a dangerous business. Quite apart from the threat
from enemy aircraft and anti-aircraft fire from the ground
(commonly known as 'Archie'), the heat and dust could badly affect
the machines, and create mechanical difficulties. Crews could be
forced to put their aircraft down in the desert. If they found a
smooth, firm and flat area, it was sometimes possible to make repairs
and take off again, or for a colleague to land and pick the pilot up
(for which task, while wounded and under fire, Lieutenant Frank
McNamara of No. 1 Squadron AFC won the VC in March 1917).
However, if the sand was soft or riddled with stones, the aircraft
could be damaged beyond repair, and then it was case of waiting for
either a British or an Ottoman patrol to pick the crew up. Often, the
Arabs could be the first on the scene, and they would then strip the

crew and 'sell' them to whichever side offered the biggest rewards.

Forced landings could be even more dangerous for the RNAS. Flight Lieutenant G.B. Dacre would record that:

> This desert flying is no joke as one depends entirely on one's engine. There is just a chance that a seaplane of our type can be landed without doing in pilot and passenger, so precautions have been taken. We take wireless, so that we can send back our position when a breakdown occurs . . . Also, we are armed and take a water bottle and food and a pocket compass. It might be possible to walk back to the coast, but walking in the wilderness where no life is to be seen is very heavy. The ship will remain off the coast for 3 days and nights, at night with a searchlight and we have Very Light [flare] pistols. It might be possible to walk to some of the camel tracks and hold up a party, pinch their camels, food and trek back to the coast. (Diary of George Dacre, FAAM)

Most of the work carried out by the flying services was reconnaissance, mapping enemy positions or movements and taking photographs of them for later analysis. These photos also allowed accurate maps to be made for the ground forces to use. Aircraft also 'spotted' for the artillery, watching the fall of shells and transmitting corrections back to the gunners to make their fire more accurate. Bombing attacks on the enemy were also increasingly undertaken. By 1918, raids against enemy headquarters, aerodromes, railways, bridges and supply dumps were a regular feature of air warfare, while bombing and strafing troops was a task throughout the war. The attacks on troops did not always do very much damage, but they had a serious effect on the morale of those underneath. Lieutenant Cedric Hill, an Australian serving with No. 14 Squadron, recorded the effect when he attacked a camp near El Arish in April 1916:

> It is lovely in the early morning flying over the desert and I had a pleasant hour and a half trouble-free flight before

sighting the camp which I could see long before I reached it. I decided to give the Turks a surprise so I sneaked up on the camp by flying very low and as I passed over it with what I hoped would be an impressive roar I dropped a bomb in the middle of it.

It was extraordinary what effect one bomb could produce. It was just like hitting a beehive with a brick. What had looked like a peaceful camp a few minutes ago was now alive with people rushing about in all directions. Judging by the various states of dress I think most of the people who popped out of the tents must have been in bed or just getting up when the bomb exploded. (Hill, *The Spook and the Commandant*, p. 40)

A basic history of the aerial campaigns can be found in Vols 5 and 6 of the official history of the RAF, *The War in the Air*, Vol. 5 (Oxford, Oxford University Press, 1935), by Captain H.A. Jones, reprints of which are available from Naval & Military Press. Details on No. 1 Squadron AFC are also in the *Australian Official History of the Great War*, Vol. VIII, *The Australian Flying Corps in the Western and Eastern Theatres of war* (Sydney, Angus and Robertson Ltd, 1923) by Frederick Cutlack, while an excellent database of all Australians who served with the flying services can be found at www.ww1aero.org.au.

For British aircrew, Chris Hobson's *Airmen Died in the Great War 1914–18: The Roll of Honour of the British & Commonwealth Air Services in the First World War* (Hayward, Naval & Military Press, 1995), provides basic biographical details. Trevor Henshaw's magnificent book *The Sky Their Battlefield* (London, Grub Street, 1995) provides a daily listing of casualties and the circumstances of their loss, although it must be said that his records for the Middle East are not nearly as comprehensive as those for the Western Front. There are some good published histories of No. 14 Squadron too, with the most recent being the first volume of Michael Napier's excellent *Winged Crusaders: The exploits of 14 Squadron RFC & RAF 1914–1945* (Barnsley, Pen & Sword Aviation, 2012). Many of the same basic records can be used to find out more about airmen as are used for soldiers, although they're usually kept in a different place. Airmen's (as RFC/RAF other ranks are known) Records of Service are held in AIR 79 at TNA, but are held in service number order. They can be searched by name and accessed through TNA themselves, or on Find My Past. Officers' Records of Service are also at TNA and accessible through Find My Past, and are held in AIR 76. A 'snap shot' of a man's service could also be found in the RAF Muster Roll, compiled on 1 April 1918, the day the RAF was formed. This lists all of the other ranks in service number order, and gives their trades and rank both under their previous service (i.e. in the RFC or RNAS) and their new ones in the RAF. It also lists when they joined the flying services, what terms they joined on ('DW' for 'Duration of War' or 'OE' for 'Ordinary Enlistment'), the date of their last promotion, and their daily rate of pay. However, it is just a snapshot of the single day, and it was not kept up to date. Copies can be seen at TNA or the RAF Museum, or can be searched and accessed through the RAF Museum's 'Storyvault' website – www.rafmuseumstoryvault.org.uk, as well as Ancestry and Find My Past.

The Storyvault also gives access to the April 1918 Air Force List, which lists officers, and various sets of what are known as 'Casualty Cards'. These are actually several sets of casualty and medical records, generally for officers and aircrew (although they are not complete) while some other ranks and ground crews are also included. These include details on accidents, wounds and losses, and a certain amount of medical information. This is an on-going project. The RAF Museum also hold files that were kept on officer's transfers and movements overseas, which at the time of writing are being conserved and digitised, and should be available soon. There are separate series of these for the Western Front and for the Middle East, and unfortunately they are not complete, but the ones that do exist list all of the movements between units of officers while overseas.

There is an excellent set of records for Australian aircrew and ground staff that has been put together by the Australian Society of WW1 Aero Historians, and can be found at www.ww1aero.org.au.

The RAF Museum also takes care of the Royal Aero Club (RAeC) collection. Until the middle of the war, pilots had to take the RAeC flying test before qualifying for their 'wings' – the military badge that showed they were qualified pilots. From 1916 onwards, taking the RAeC test became less common, but many still did. The RAeC kept a card index of all of the flying licences that they issued, including the date, place and aeroplane used to take the test, as well as the basic biographical details of the licensee. Each licence had a photo of the pilot in it, and a master set of these were kept by the RAeC. Some volumes have been lost, but most survive and are held, along with the licence cards, by the RAF Museum. The cards can also be accessed through Ancestry.

Just as with the army, RFC and later RAF units kept a War Diary, which can be found at TNA in AIR 1. This should record the same sort of details as the army War Diary, with the addition of flights made. There are various miscellaneous files relating to most of the squadrons in Egypt and Palestine in AIR 1 as well, but these vary in extent and content between units. Sometimes reports on individual sorties, raids or aerial engagements can be found, as can correspondence files relating to officers serving with the squadrons. These sometimes include details on casualties, and correspondence between the commanding officer and the next of kin of those who were killed. AIR 1 is a bit of a mess with little overall structure, so it is best to have a good look on the Discovery online catalogue rather than just scrolling through the listings.

Records on RNAS personnel are included among the RAF records where the personnel transferred to that organisation when it was formed. For the men who served before that, the officers' Records of Service are held in ADM 273 and those for other ranks are in ADM 188, both at TNA. Operational records are in ADM 137, although some are also held by the Fleet Air Arm Museum at Yeovilton. Records of casualties are held in ADM 242, which is also available through Find My Past.

The RN and other maritime forces played an important role in the Egypt and Palestine campaigns – after all, one of the main points

Members of the RFC pose for a studio photograph.

of the campaigns was to protect the waterway of the Suez Canal. In the early months of the war, the RN was busy in tracking down and rounding up German and Austrian (and later Ottoman) merchant shipping, seizing the ships to not only deny their use to the enemy, but also to add them to Britain's own merchant fleet. British merchant ships came in and out of Egypt in a constant stream. Some just passed through the Canal and kept going, part of the endless effort to transport raw materials to the war industries in not only Britain, but also France and Italy (whose own merchant fleets were too small to keep up with demand). Others sailed to or from Egypt bringing in supplies to the EEF, or taking material out again to supply the forces in Gallipoli and Salonika.

This mass of merchant traffic became an increasingly tempting and important target for the enemy, and by the middle of 1915 German and Austrian submarines were active in the Mediterranean. As their efforts escalated, reaching their peak in 1917, so the number of ships of the RN and other Allied nations (including Japan) in the Mediterranean grew, operating from or regularly visiting Egyptian ports. Escorting these merchant ships became a major effort, and many British civilian ships including trawlers and even ferries were requisitioned to aid the effort, often operated by their pre-war crews.

Coastal patrols also remained important throughout the war, with British and French warships constantly monitoring the enemy coastline, and escorting the seaplane carriers that allowed reconnaissance and bombing raids deep inland. In the Red Sea, the navy provided crucial support to the Arab Revolt.

Rather than War Diaries, the RN maintained Ship's Logs, which were the daily account of the movements and actions for the ship. For surface vessels, these are held at TNA in ADM 53, and for submarines in ADM 173. The records of service of RN officers and Warrant Officers are in ADM 196, and those for the other ranks (known as 'ratings') are in ADM 188. However, the navy also had a bewildering array of sub-categories including the RN Volunteer Reserve, the RN Reserve and the Royal Fleet Auxiliary, while the Mercantile Marine (operating merchant ships) was a separate entity.

These are too complex to explore here, and you are recommended to obtain expert advice, such as from Simon Fowler's *Tracing Your Naval Ancestors* (Barnsley, Pen & Sword, 2011).

HOW THEY FOUGHT: IMPERIAL CAMEL CORPS

Britain had raised camel units to serve in campaigns in Egypt and the Sudan before, in the 1880s and 1890s, but a shortage of camels in the country after the start of the First World War meant that none were raised again until November 1915. Then, companies of camel troops (or 'cameliers') were raised to serve in the Western Desert against the Senussi. Camels could go for four or five days without water, while carrying much heavier loads than horses, allowing the troops to carry enough water, food and extra ammunition to survive for that long themselves. This allowed them to make long patrols deep into the desert, as they would later do in the Sinai Peninsula. This area, south of the Sinai Desert, was peppered with religious sites, the European monks and nuns at which acted as an intelligence network for the British by gathering information from passing pilgrims. These detachments monitoring the peninsula were known as the 'Pilgrim Patrol'.

Several camel companies were pulled together to serve as a single unit during the Battle of Romani in August 1916, but a properly organised Imperial Camel Corps was not established until January 1917. Then, four battalions were formed. They were Mounted Infantry, organised like infantry battalions with 4 companies of about 200 men. Two of the battalions were drawn from the ALH, one was recruited half from the Australians and half from the New Zealand Mounted Rifles, and one (which was larger, with six companies) from British Yeomanry units. Every man was a volunteer, and the Brigade tended to appeal to the more daring, or reckless, soldier. Many were drawn by the adventure and glamour of being in such a unit, although most lost

A member of the Bikaner Camel Corps, showing the equipment carried by a 'camelier'.

at least some of their ardour when they first encountered their camels. Most cavalrymen form a close bond with their mounts, but the camels were a far cry from their beloved horses, not least in appearance:

> The Arabs say that at the Creation, when the beasts of the earth were formed, there were left over a lot of remnants out of which was made a camel, and the parts are not hard to find. The head of a sheep was placed on the neck of a giraffe, which was attached to the body of a cow, and the neck bent itself in shame at being put to such a use. The tail of an ass was appended, and the whole was set on the legs of a horse, which ended in the pads of a dog, on each of which was stuck the claw of an ostrich, and the monstrosity,

evidently being considered a failure, was banished to live in the desert where no other quadruped could exist, and where its solitary existence gave it 'the hump'. (J. Robertson, *With the Cameliers in Palestine* (n.p., Anthony Rowe Ltd, 1938), p. 35)

Australian Oliver Hogue found that the initial revulsion did slowly wear off:

We hated the thought of 'em. We hated the sight of 'em. We hated the smell of 'em. We hated the shape of 'em. The very idea of association with such brutes was hateful to us – at first.

But the time was not far distant when we were to forget all our initial antipathies. Familiarity bred content. The law of compensation was in operation. A beast with so many obvious vices as a camel must have some compensating virtues. But it *did* take time to unearth them. (O. Hogue, *The Cameliers* (n.p., Leonaur Ltd, 2008), p. 15)

The different battalions and companies often worked independently of each other on long patrols or raids, but when a major action or campaign was expected three of the battalions would be brought together to form the Imperial Camel Corps Brigade, while the fourth maintained their usual patrol areas or rested. They could hold outposts on the front line just like any infantry, as the 1st (Australian) Battalion did in the Jordan Valley when they were attacked in April 1918. A ferocious Ottoman bombardment and infantry attack saw all of the officers and most of the men killed and wounded, and they had to resort to rolling boulders down the hillside as ammunition ran low. They held all day until relieved, and the post was renamed 'The Camel's Hump' in their honour.

Only occasionally did the units fight on camelback, as when one patrol came across an Ottoman column by surprise:

Two days [after the Battle of Romani] an incident occurred which was described in one of the London papers as a mounted charge by the Imperial Camel Corps. What actually happened was this. The Camel Corps scouts suddenly came upon a small enemy ammunition and baggage column consisting of thirty pack mules, a troop of cavalry and about eighty dismounted men, who were crossing an open stretch of ground. The Camel Corps had part of two companies, approximately seventy men in all, a third of whom were ordered to dismount and give covering fire while the remainder, taking advantage of the confusion, charged in extended formation, yelling and firing their rifles from the saddle in the approved Arab style. Needless to say they did not hit anything but, although the Turks put up some slight resistance and managed to get some of their pack animals away, most of them were finally rounded up and surrendered. (G. Inchbald, *With the Imperial Camel Corps in the Great War* (n.p., Leanaur Ltd, 2005), p. 108)

The camels did less well in the mountains of central and northern Palestine than they had in the desert, and in June 1918 it was decided to split up the Imperial Camel Corps. The British 2nd Battalion was retained, with two of its companies and most of the Brigade's camels being transferred to operate with T.E. Lawrence in supporting the Arab Revolt, where they conducted raids on the Hejaz Railway. The remainder was formed into the 5th Australian Light Horse Brigade, with the New Zealand contingent acting as their machine-gun squadron, continuing to fight with distinction until the Ottoman surrender in October 1918.

Chapter 9

VISITING THE BATTLEFIELDS TODAY

The battlefields of the Egypt and Palestine campaigns are not always very easy to visit today. Egypt has been in a state of flux since the Arab Spring of 2011. It is best to visit on organised tours, which will cover the main cities such as Alexandria and Cairo, and perhaps Port Said and parts of the Suez Canal. There is not much to see from the First World War these days but at least you can visit places where the troops would have been and marvel at some of the same sites that they saw. The Great Pyramids at Giza, for example, were the site of an Australian training camp, as if any excuse is needed to visit an already truly spectacular place. Being on an organised tour ensures security, and also avoids the considerable dangers of trying to drive in Egypt.

Travelling out into the Sinai Desert to visit some of the battlefields is not recommended. The northern Sinai is the home to various militant dissident groups, and the area is the scene of regular military activity by the government. At the time of writing, the Foreign and Commonwealth Office (FCO) advises against any travel in that region, and that is unlikely to change in the near future.

Most of the sites from the Palestine campaign are safer, or at least those that fall within modern Israel. Gaza, for example, is not a safe place to visit and the FCO advises against it, and the old battlefields are now mostly built over anyway. At the other end of the line, Beersheba (Be'er Sheva) is a pleasant city to visit, with plenty of First World War related sites. The Park of the Australian Soldier contains a spectacular statue to commemorate the ALH's role in capturing the city. In the centre of the old city, the Ottoman governor's house is now the Negev Museum of Modern Art, and on the same square is Allenby Park with a bust of the general on a plinth. (There is also, on the corner diagonally opposite the Museum, an excellent falafel and pitta kiosk.) A short walk from here is the CWGC Cemetery, and the old Ottoman railway station, now restored. Next to the station is a memorial to the Ottoman troops killed there.

On the outskirts of the city, you can visit the site of the Australian charge near an old railway bridge, and the site at Tel el Saba, which was the key to the Ottoman defensive positions and is an interesting archaeological site as well. Half an hour south of the city you can visit the old British wells at Bir Asluj (now Golda Meir Park), and further south still the remains of a bridge at Mashabim Junction, blown up by an Australian raid in May 1917. Between Gaza and Beersheba runs the ANZAC Trail, which is well worth taking a day to follow. It includes the ANZAC Memorial (overlooking Gaza) and the high ground at Tel Gamma and Tel el Fara (both used as bases for operations, and affording excellent views), and also the restored portion of railway at Besor Park, which is close to the springs and other interesting remains at Shellal.

Jerusalem is always worth a visit, and can form a useful base for exploring most of Israel. The city itself contains numerous memorials and cemeteries, including the excellent main Jerusalem War Cemetery and Memorial to the Missing. There are also other memorials around the city to the 60th (London) Division and the Egyptian Labour Corps. Also make time to visit the Jaffa Gate, the place where Allenby entered the city, and the steps of the Barbican where he read his Proclamation are just around the corner.

From Jerusalem it is easy to hire a car and reach various sites where British troops fought, including Nabi Samwil, and the Mount of Olives. The main road to Tel Aviv, Route 1, roughly follows the line of the British advance on Jerusalem and driving down it gives a feel of what a truly rugged region this is. The height and steepness of many of the mountains has to be seen to be believed. Nearer the coast there is a memorial to the 155th Brigade, 52nd (Lowland)

The 'Allenby Memorial' in Jerusalem, actually dedicated to the 60th (London) Division, on the site where the Mayor of Jerusalem surrendered the city.

Division, near the Nahr el Auja, and one to the New Zealand Mounted Rifles at Ayun Kara, near Richon Le Zion.

Incidentally, driving around Israel, and Jerusalem in particular, can be a bit of an experience. Generally, the motorways are well signposted, but in towns and cities street signs can be hard to spot. They are usually bi-lingual and sometimes tri-lingual, making the print small enough to be difficult to read as you drive past. Good maps are essential, but bear in mind that maps and street signs do not always match up exactly, depending on the translations. You may find that other drivers are quite energetic in their approach to the roads (although in fairness they are tame compared with Egyptian drivers), particularly on the West Bank. Give buses as wide a berth as possible if you value your rental car deposit.

It is also possible to get onto an organised trip from Jerusalem to Bethlehem, which is within the Palestinian zone and cannot be visited by a private individual in a hire car. You can easily get into the Jordan Valley too, which is quite spectacular, although you may need to pass through one or more military checkpoints where you will need to show your passport, and you need to remain aware that this is a militarily sensitive area.

In fact, wherever you go in Israel you will see a heavy military presence. Troops are everywhere. Even if, as is often the case, they are on leave or off duty, they are usually armed. It can take a little getting used to. Technically, it is illegal to take photographs of the military in Israel, but for the most part the law is not enforced as it is almost impossible not to include at least some in every shot. That said, you are best not taking photographs of guard posts, checkpoints and other fixed defences.

Further north, Nazareth is a predominantly Arab town, but unlike Bethlehem it is not in the Palestinian Authority areas and there are no restrictions on travel. In the centre of the city is the Casa Nova Hotel, opposite the Church of the Annunciation. This was the site of the main Ottoman headquarters in September 1918, and this area was fought over during the cavalry raid on 21 September.

From Nazareth, you can go either north-west to Haifa, where the modern city is almost unrecognisable as the hamlet of 1918 but does contain a CWGC cemetery, or north-east to the Sea of Galilee. Here a few sites are identifiable from the 1918 campaign, and it is also an incredibly beautiful area, especially in the autumn when the flowers are in bloom.

Travelling much further north than there is inadvisable, due to the political and military situation in Syria.

The Society for the Heritage of World War 1 in Israel can provide valuable travel advice: www.ww1-israel.org.

HOW THEY FOUGHT: ARMOURED CARS

Armoured cars were a brand new weapon in the First World War, and far more widely used than their more famous sibling, the tank. The first armoured cars in Egypt were the Royal Naval Armoured Car Division (RNACD). The RN had pioneered the use of armoured cars in Belgium in 1914, and then deployed several units to Gallipoli, where they were mostly used as static machine-gun posts. However, when the conflict with the Senussi broke out in November 1915 the Emergency Squadron of the RNACD was on hand and was quickly deployed to the Western Desert. It consisted of six Rolls-Royce armoured cars, plus about twenty support vehicles to carry stores, spare parts and mechanics, and included two trucks fitted with wireless sets and an ambulance.

The RN's armoured cars were being transferred to the army at this time, and the Emergency Squadron was transferred across by the end of the year. Under the army, the armoured car force in Egypt was expanded to several Light Armoured Car Batteries or Light Armoured Motor Batteries, still using Rolls-Royce cars. These were based on the chassis of Rolls-Royce Silver Ghosts with armoured plates forming the body work. The sections around the engine were hinged so that they could be folded back to keep the engine cool when not in action. Each had a rotating turret with a single Maxim machine gun mounted in it, and which could be

A Rolls-Royce Armoured Car in the mountains of northern Palestine.

removed to either lighten the car or make it more suitable for reconnaissance work. Otherwise, visibility from the car was pretty poor, with the driver and gunner only having small slits to look through. There was a hatch on top of the turret that could be opened to allow a better view or more air flow into the stifling metal body, and there was also a small platform at the back of the car, where the boot would usually be. A crewman (or other passenger) could sit or stand on this while travelling, or it could be used to hold extra stores for long patrols. The crew was nominally three men – a driver and two gunners (one to fire the gun, one to feed in the ammunition) – but one of the gunners was often left behind due to the extremely cramped conditions inside the car.

The cars packed a powerful punch, especially when used in patrols of two or three cars, and they could be very fast, but they had limitations. On rough desert roads the driver had to be very careful to avoid rocks or stones that could burst a tyre (each car was often fitted with two tyres on each hub, so that if one burst in action they could still drive), or puncture some vital part underneath the car. Even at slow speeds they could cover vast distances, as apart from occasional refuelling there was no need to stop and rest as with men or horses. Being so powerfully armed, they were popular as scouts (ranging ahead along roads in Palestine, for example, during the advance of the winter of 1917), or for patrolling in areas such as the Western Desert where supplying larger forces would be a problem. Lawrence of Arabia also made great use of them in the last eighteen months of war, again utilising their speed and firepower to provide a significant 'punch' for his Arab forces.

In action, the inside of the cars could be appalling. Sam Rolls drove his car against the Senussi, and later with Lawrence:

> The reek of burnt cordite, blending with the stench of our hot, sweating bodies, made us gasp for fresh air, but with the armour lid closed down there was little chance of getting any. The heat, a combination of that given out by the racing engine and that of the sun on the steel cylinder, added to the din of the stuttering gun and the clatter of the ammunition belts, made the conditions nerve-shattering. Hot, empty cartridge cases frequently fell on my bare neck, and into my shirt, stinging my flesh; and the general sensation inside our war chariot was infernal. (S.C. Rolls, *Steel chariots in the desert* (n.p., Leonaur Ltd, 2005), p. 34)

Unarmoured cars were also widely used, known at various times as Light Car Patrols or Motor Machine Gun Batteries. These generally were based around six cars, which were converted Model T Fords. They had no extra armour, and were typically in a 'flatbed' configuration with a platform running back from behind the front seats. They could be fitted with heavy or light machine guns, or the space could be piled with stores for a long patrol. As with the armoured cars, they were frequently used for long patrols in areas with a particularly hostile environment, or for scouting ahead of the army.

CHRONOLOGY

1 August 1914	Germany and the Ottoman Empire sign a secret treaty.
4 August 1914	Britain declares war on Germany.
8 September 1914	Indian troops start arriving in Egypt.
27 September 1914	42nd (East Lancashire) Division begins arriving in Egypt.
29 October 1914	The Ottoman Empire attacks Russia.
2 November 1914	Martial Law declared in Egypt, with Major General Sir John Maxwell effectively running the country.
3 November 1914	RN warships bombard Ottoman forts on the Dardanelles.
5 November 1914	Britain declares war on the Ottoman Empire.
17 November 1914	The first detachment of the RFC arrives in Egypt.
3 December 1914	The first convoy of Anzac troops arrives in Egypt.
18 December 1914	Egypt declared a British Protectorate.
14 January 1915	Ottoman forces leave Beersheba to attack the Suez Canal.
3 February 1915	Battle of the Suez Canal.
25 April 1915	British landings in the Dardanelles mark the start of the Gallipoli campaign.
5 November 1915	German submarine *U-35* sinks HMS *Tara*, and hands the prisoners over to the Senussi. *U-35* then bombards British and Egyptian forces at Sollum.
20 November 1915	The Western Frontier Force formed to fight the Senussi.

22 November 1915	Egyptian Coastguard bases at Sidi Barani and Baqbaq abandoned to the Senussi.
23 November 1915	Egyptian Coastguard base at Sollum abandoned to the Senussi.
11 December 1915	British column ambushed by the Senussi at Wadi Senab.
13 December 1915	British column ambushed by the Senussi at Wadi Hasheifiat.
20 December 1915	British and Anzac troops withdrawn from Suvla Bay and Anzac Cove on the Gallipoli Peninsula.
25 December 1915	British forces attack the Senussi camp at Jebel Medwa/Wadi Majid.
8 January 1916	British forces withdrawn from Cape Helles, marking the end of the Gallipoli campaign.
23 January 1916	British forces attack the Senussi camp at Halazin.
February 1916	Work begins on a railway into the Sinai Desert, to supply British forces once the advance begins. A pipeline soon follows, although work on this is slower.
26 February 1916	British forces attack the Senussi camp at Agagia.
10 March 1916	The military governor in Egypt, Major General Sir John Maxwell, is recalled to the UK. Lieutenant General Sir Archibald Murray, previously commander of the Mediterranean Expeditionary Force in Gallipoli, is placed in command of all forces in Egypt. These are now to be known as the Egyptian Expeditionary Force.
14 March 1916	British forces retake Sollum, and then attack a Senussi camp at Bir 'Aziz.
17 March 1916	An armoured car column rescues the survivors from HMS *Tara*.

23 April 1916	5th Mounted Brigade takes heavy casualties at Qatia and Oghratina stopping an Ottoman force from attacking the Suez Canal.
5 June 1916	Opening shots of the Arab Revolt.
9 July 1916	Arab forces capture Mecca.
3–5 August 1916	British victory in the Battle of Romani.
20 October 1916	British forces reoccupy Bahariya and Dakhla oases in the Western Desert.
23 December 1916	British forces capture Ottoman garrison at El Magdhaba.
9 January 1917	British forces capture Ottoman garrison at El Magruntein (Rafa).
3 February 1917	A British armoured car force recaptures Siwa Oasis, the last Senussi stronghold in Egypt.
26–7 March 1917	British defeat at the 1st Battle of Gaza.
17–19 April 1917	British defeat at the 2nd Battle of Gaza.
27 June 1917	General Sir Edmund Allenby replaces General Sir Archibald Murray as commander of the EEF.
6 July 1917	Arab forces seize Aqaba.
27 October 1917	Start of artillery bombardment on Gaza.
31 October 1917	XX Corps and Desert Mounted Corps take Beersheba.
2 November 1917	XXI Corps attack Gaza.
3 November 1917	Break out from Beersheba begins.
7 November 1917	British find that the Ottomans have evacuated Gaza, and occupy it.
7–8 November 1917	British force a crossing on the Wadi Hesi.
11–13 November 1917	British break through the defensive line around Junction Station, particularly El Tine and El Mughar Ridge.
12 November 1917	Ottoman counter-attack at Balin, halted by Australian Mounted Division.
14 November 1917	British capture Junction Station.

18 November 1917	British resume attacks, XX Corps north to capture Jaffa and XXI Corps east into the Judean Mountains.
21 November 1917	British forces attack Nabi Samwil, just west of Jerusalem and overlooking the main approaches to the Holy City. Heavy fighting continues for several weeks, with heavy casualties on both sides.
24–5 November 1917	XX Corps attacks across the Nahr el Auja River, north of Jaffa, but is forced to retreat.
25 November 1917	XXI Corps halts its advance in the Judean Mountains.
27 November– 1 December 1917	Ottoman forces make several counter-attacks west of Jerusalem. The British hold, while XX Corps replaces XXI Corps.
8 December 1917	XX Corps begins their advance on Jerusalem. The Ottomans evacuate the city that night.
9 December 1917	British forces enter Jerusalem.
11 December 1917	Official surrender of Jerusalem to General Allenby. Advance continues north and west of the city.
20–2 December 1917	XXI Corps crosses the Nahr el Auja, advancing several miles and making the port at Jaffa secure for use.
27 December 1917	Ottoman forces make counter-attacks north of Jerusalem. The British defeat the attacks, and then advance themselves.
30 December 1917	Both sides cease operations.
19 February 1918	XX Corps advances into the Jordan Valley.
21 February 1918	XX Corps occupies Jericho.
8–12 March 1918	British push north from Jerusalem.
21 March– 12 April 1918	1st Es Salt/Amman Raid.
11 April 1918	Ottoman counter-attacks on Ghoraniyeh Bridgehead, across the River Jordan.

30 April–4 May 1918	2nd Es Salt/Amman Raid.
April–June 1918	Extensive transfer of British troops from Palestine to France, and replacement with Indian troops.
19 September 1918	EEF launch Battle of Megiddo, advancing north towards Syria.
20 September 1918	British cavalry raid on the Ottoman headquarters at Nazareth. Ottoman lines are broken in the Battle of Sharon (on the coast) and Battle of Mount Ephraim (Judean Mountains).
21 September 1918	RAF destroys the remains of the Ottoman 7th Army in the Wadi Fara.
23 September 1918	British forces capture Acre and Haifa.
24 September 1918	Australian cavalry reach Sea of Galilee.
25 September 1918	British forces capture Amman.
27 September 1918	Arab forces capture Deraa.
1 October 1918	British and Arab forces take Damascus.
8 October 1918	Indian troops take Beirut.
13 October 1918	British forces take Tripolis.
15 October 1918	British forces take Homs.
25 October 1918	Arab forces reach Aleppo.
26 October 1918	British forces reach Aleppo.
30 October 1918	Ottoman Empire signs an Armistice.
March–July 1919	Egyptian Revolt.

FURTHER READING

WEBSITES
Ancestry UK: www.ancestry.co.uk
Archives New Zealand: http://archives.govt.nz
Army Service Numbers: http://armyservicenumbers.blogspot.co.uk
Auckland War Memorial Museum's Cenotaph Database:
   www.aucklandmuseum.com/war-memorial/online-cenotaph
Australian Light Horse Association: www.lighthorse.org.au
Australian Light Horse Studies Centre: http://alh-
   research.tripod.com
Australian Society of WW1 Aero Historians: www.ww1aero.org.au
Australian War Memorial: www.awm.gov.au
Find My Past: www.findmypast.co.uk
Great War Forum: http://1914-1918.invasionzone.com
Imperial War Museum: www.iwm.org.uk
National Army Museum: www.nam.ac.uk
Naval & Military Archive: www.nmarchive.com
Naval & Military Press: www.naval-military-press.com
New Zealand History Net: www.nzhistory.net
New Zealand Mounted Rifles: www.nzmr.org
RAF Museum Storyvault: www.rafmuseumstoryvault.org.uk
RAF Museum: www.rafmuseum.org
Records of Service still held by the MoD:
   www.gov.uk/guidance/requests-for-personal-data-and-service-
   records
Scotlands People: www.scotlandspeople.gov.uk
Society for the Heritage of World War 1 in Israel: www.ww1-
   israel.org
South African Military History Society:
   http://samilitaryhistory.org/index.html
The Long Long Trail: www.longlongtrail.co.uk

The National Archives: www.nationalarchives.gov.uk
UK Probate Office: www.gov.uk/wills-probate-
  inheritance/searching-for-probate-records
Western Front Association: www.westernfrontassociation.com

There are also some useful Facebook sites, where information can
  be sought or exchanged:
'Egyptian Expeditionary Force in WW1' (run by the author)
'Descendents of PoW in Ottoman hands in WW1 (Esir Torunlari)'
'Fighting "Johnny Turk": The Great War in Egypt, Palestine and
  Mesopotamia'

BOOKS AND OTHER SOURCES

Various sources are quoted in the text. Those with references
starting 'IWM' followed by a number are items held by the
Imperial War Museum. 'FAAM' denotes the Fleet Air Arm
Museum at Yeovilton. Other items marked 'QOWH' are from the
Museum of the Queen's Own Worcestershire Hussars (Yeomanry).

The books cited and some additional recommendations are:

1/1st Hants Royal Horse Artillery (2005), Uckfield, Naval & Military
  Press
5th Battalion Highland Light Infantry (1921), Glasgow, MacLehose,
  Jackson & Co.
Allenby, General Sir E.H.H. (1919), *A brief record of the advance of
  the Egyptian Expeditionary Force*, London, HMSO
Anglesey, Marques (1994), *A history of the British Cavalry 1816–
  1919*, Vol. 5, *Egypt, Palestine and Syria 1914 to 1919*, London, Leo
  Cooper
Badcock, Lieutenant Colonel G.E. (1925), *A history of the Transport
  Services of the Egyptian Expeditionary Force, 1916–1917–1918*,
  London, Hugh Rees Limited
Barr, J. (2006), *Setting the desert on fire: T. E. Lawrence and Britain's
  secret war in Arabia, 1916–18*, London, Bloomsbury

Bluett, A. (2007), *A Gunner's Crusade*, n.p., Leonaur Ltd

Bruce, A. (2002), *The last crusade: The Palestine campaign in the First World War*, London, John Murray Ltd

Burrows, J.W. (1931), *The Essex Regiment: Essex Territorial Infantry Brigade (4th, 5th, 6th and 7th Battalions)*, Southend-on-Sea, Essex Territorial Army Association

'C' (1926), *The Yeomanry Cavalry of Worcestershire, 1914–1922*, Stourbridge, Mark & Moody Ltd

Clunie, K. and Austin, R. (eds) (2009), *From Gallipoli to Palestine: The War Writings of Sergeant G. T. Clunie of the Wellington Mounted Rifles, 1914–1919*, McCrae, Australia, Slouch Hat Publications

Cutlack, F.M. (1923), *Australian Official History of the Great War*, Vol. VIII, *The Australian Flying Corps in the Western and Eastern Theatres of War*, Sydney, Angus and Robertson Ltd

Dalbiac, Colonel P.H. (1927), *History of the 60th Division (2/2nd London Division)*, London, George Allen & Unwin Ltd

Dudley Ward, Major C.H. DSO MC (1921), *Regimental Records of the Royal Welch Fusiliers*, Vol. IV, *Turkey – Bulgaria – Austria*, London, Foster Groom & Co. Ltd

—— (1922), *The 74th (Yeomanry) Division in Syria and France*, London, John Murray

—— (1927), *History of the 53rd (Welsh) Division (T.F.) 1914–1918*, Cardiff, Western Mail Limited

Falls, Captain C. (1930), *Military Operations: Egypt and Palestine*, Vol. 2, London, HMSO

Fowler, S. (2011), *Tracing Your Naval Ancestors*, Barnsley, Pen & Sword

Gibbons, Lieutenant Colonel T. DSO (1921), *With the 1/5th Essex in the East*, Colchester, Benham and Company Limited

Gliddon, G. (2005), *VCs of the First World War: The Sideshows*, Stroud, Sutton Publishing

Godrich, V. (2011), *Mountains of Moab: The diary of a cavalryman with the Queen's Own Worcestershire Hussars, 1908–1919*, Dr John Godrich

Gullett, H.S. (1923), *Official history of Australia in the War of 1914–*

18, Vol. 7, *The AIF in Sinai and Palestine, 1914–18,* Sydney, Angus and Robertson Ltd

Hadaway, S. (2014), *Pyramids and Fleshpots: The Egyptian, Senussi and Eastern Mediterranean Campaigns, 1914–16,* Stroud, The History Press

—— (2015), *From Gaza to Jerusalem: The Campaign for Southern Palestine 1917,* Stroud, The History Press

Hamilton, P.M. OBE (1995), *Riders of destiny: The 4th Australian Light Horse Field Ambulance 1917–18,* Gardenvale, Mostly Unsung Military History

Hatton, S.F. (1930), *The Yarn of a Yeoman,* Uckfield, Naval & Military Press Ltd

Henshaw, Trevor (1995), *The Sky Their Battlefield,* London, Grub Street

Hill, Group Captain C.W. (1975), *The Spook and the Commandant,* London, William Kimber & Co. Ltd

Hobson, Chris (1995), *Airmen Died in the Great War 1914–18: The Roll of Honour of the British & Commonwealth Air Services in the First World War,* Hayward, Naval & Military Press

Hogue, O. (2008), *The Cameliers,* n.p., Leonaur Ltd

Inchbald, G. (2005,) *With the Imperial Camel Corps in the Great War,* n.p., Leanaur Ltd

Jones, Elias (1919), *The Road to En-Dor,* London, Bodley Head Ltd

Jones, Captain H.A. (1935), *The War in the Air,* Vol. 5, Oxford, Oxford University Press

Knight, J. (2005), *The Civil Service Rifles in the Great War: 'All Bloody Gentlemen',* Barnsley, Pen & Sword Military

Lawrence, T.E. (1979), *Seven Pillars of Wisdom,* London, Penguin Books Ltd

Mackie, J.H.F. (ed.) (2002), *Answering the call: Letters from the Somerset Light Infantry, 1914–1919,* Eggleston, Raby Books

McGuirk, R. (2007), *The Sanusi's Little War,* London, Arabian Publishing

MacMunn, Lieutenant General Sir G. KCB KCSI DSO and Captain C. Falls (1928), *Military Operations: Egypt and Palestine,* Vol. 1, London, HMSO

Moore, Lieutenant A.B. (1920), *The Mounted Rifleman in Sinai and Palestine,* Auckland, Whitcombe & Tombs Ltd

Napier, Michael (2012), *Winged Crusaders: The exploits of 14 Squadron RFC & RAF 1914–1945,* Barnsley, Pen & Sword Aviation

Nicol, Sergeant C.G. (1921), *The story of two campaigns: Official war history of the Auckland Mounted Rifles Regiment, 1914–1919,* Auckland, Wilson & Hooton

Powell, A. (2009), *Women in the war zone: Hospital Service in World War 1,* Stroud, The History Press

Powles, Colonel C.G. CMG DSO (ed.) (1928), *The history of the Canterbury Mounted Rifles, 1914–19,* Auckland, Whitcombe & Tombs Ltd

Preston, Lieutenant Colonel The Hon. R.M.P. DSO (1921), *The Desert Mounted Corps: An account of the cavalry operations in Palestine and Syria, 1917–1918,* London, Constable and Company Limited

Robertson, J. (1938), *With the Cameliers in Palestine,* n.p., Anthony Rowe Ltd

Rolls, S.C. (2005), *Steel chariots in the desert,* n.p., Leonaur Ltd

Sutherland, L.W. (1936), *Aces and Kings,* London, John Hamilton

Teichman, Captain O. DSO MC (1921), *The diary of a Yeomanry M.O.,* London, T. Fisher Unwin Ltd

Thompson, Lieutenant Colonel R.R. (1923), *The Fifty-Second Lowland Division 1914–1918,* Glasgow, Maclehose, Jackson & Co.

Wilkie, Major A.J. (1924), *The official war history of the Wellington Mounted Rifles Regiment 1914–1919,* Auckland, Whitcombe and Tombs Limited

Wilson, R. (1987), *Palestine 1917,* Tunbridge Wells, D.J. Costello (Publishers) Ltd

Woodward, D.R. (2007), *Forgotten soldiers of the First World War,* Stroud, Tempus Publishing Ltd

INDEX